By the same author

The Business of Integrity

Travelling between handbags

S.U.I.T.S.™ Tailor-made personal branding for iconic leadership

MATT WHITE

S.U.I.T.S™

TAILOR-MADE PERSONAL BRANDING FOR ICONIC LEADERSHIP

MATT WHITE

ST PAUL
&JOHN
PUBLISHERS

ST. PAUL & JOHN PUBLISHERS

First published in South Africa in 2017 by St. Paul and John Publishers
in Paperback

ST. PAUL & JOHN PUBLISHERS is a subsidiary of MATT WHITE International

First Edition 2017

The publisher apologises for any errors or omissions and would be grateful
to be notified of any corrections that should be incorporated in future
additions of this book.

Set in 9,5pt Droid Serif
Typeset by Hesti Steenkamp, For the Love of Ginger, Pretoria, South Africa
Front cover design by Michael Healy, www.michaelthomas.co.za
Back cover design by Hesti Steenkamp
Photo credit: Anna J. Nel, www.annajphoto.co.za
Printed in South Africa by Business Print

A CIP catalogue record for this book is available from
the National Library of South Africa

Paperback ISBN 978-0-620-57898-1

St Paul & John Publishers is committed to a sustainable future for our
business, our readers and our planet. This book is printed on Kami,
woodfree natural cream bond, 80gsm.

Publisher's Legal Disclaimer

This book presents a wide range of opinions related to health and well-being, including certain ideas, treatments, and procedures that may be hazardous or illegal without proper medical supervision. These opinions reflect the research and ideas of the author and those whose ideas the author presents, but are not intended to substitute the services of a trained healthcare practitioner. Consult with your healthcare practitioner before engaging in any diet, drug, or exercise regimen. The author and the publisher disclaim responsibility for any effects, adverse or otherwise, resulting directly or indirectly from information obtained in this book.

Author's Disclaimer

I am many things to many people; what I'm not is a medical or psychological practitioner. I practice branding. I have chosen the best set of tools in my kit to help you understand and to support you in the creation of your brand. In the context of personal branding, I will refer to the business of branding and to medical and psychological constructs as I understand and use them, based on my training.

The examples in the stories I tell and the applications I present in no way constitute the diagnosis or prognosis of a medical or psychological condition. Rather, they are a set of challenges that I pose in the form of questions or statements, giving you an alternative viewpoint from which to explore your territory.

You are the expert in You.

In this piece of work, I presuppose that you're capable of making informed decisions and engineering subsequent actions that will serve you and the world at large in a context that makes a better world for all.

Take care of yourself during your journey, and avoid doing anything stupid. It wouldn't make for a good brand experience for you or me. Consult a medical doctor, a lawyer, and a common-sense specialist before doing anything in this book.

To you, who is crazy enough to think you can change the world, because you will.

"Whom shall I send, and who will go for Us?"
Then I said, "Here am I. Send me!"

MATT WHITE

S.U.I.T.S ™ - TAILOR-MADE PERSONAL BRANDING FOR ICONIC LEADERSHIP

ESTABLISH YOUR PERSONAL BRAND AND LIVE A LEGENDARY LIFE.

INTRODUCTION

Game rules for successful personal branding

> *"If you don't like change, you are going to like irrelevance even less".*
>
> **– Tom Peters –**

So many people "dream" about having a successful brand... you are now in the process of "creating" that. Congratulations!

You are both the architect and the resident of your brand, and I am both inspired and excited about that!

I'm thrilled that you've decided to use the S.U.I.T.S.™ Model as your design; create and implement your brand, and I will do my best to ensure this memorable and practical experience gets you closer to the success that you want and deserve.

You can look forward to being challenged and to receiving a mountain of information and my support as you work hard and embrace all that you are.

Remember that I'm here to serve you.

Branding as an Iconic Leader

Leadership, like many constructs, has contextual definitions. To achieve the 'Iconic Leader' status, one must successfully establish in the audience's mind his or her significant edge for setting and achieving visionary accomplishments and continually delivering on promises. It is fair to define an Iconic Leader with a powerful personal brand as one who wields competence, is committed to action, creates contexts within which others can become all they can be, and establishes a culture of connection with compassion for themselves and those who invest trust in them.

These leadership achievements are mostly possible through the successful delivery and implementation of a collection of differentiated soft and hard products and services that are significantly unusual. Who you are and who you want to be are only valuable if what you desire and what your audience perceives you to be are the same thing.

You can't be all things to all people. But, with key foundations and deliverables in place, you can be all that you are and want to be in the minds of your stakeholders, consumers, and those with whom you are in relationships.

Using S.U.I.T.S.™ will enable you to create a logo, define your online activities, and create and maintain the relationships you want through the uniquely designed packaging and communication of your products and services.

The S.U.I.T.S.™ model will further support you in the creation of a brand strategy regarding how, what, where, when, and with whom you plan to engage. This will culminate in a reinforced advertising, communication, and distribution channel strategy that will include your visual and verbal presentation of yourself.

Finally, you will unlock your intrinsic brand equity through the emotional connection you build with your audience, enabling you to create emotional, financial, relational, and physical wealth.

Your S.U.I.T.S.™ Personal Brand journey will be a business of self-discovery. You may find it challenging, even overwhelming, time-intensive, and uncomfortable. I promise that all the hard work will be worth it when you explore your mission in life, the benefits and features of your products and services, your ideal audience's perception of you, and the qualities its members want to associate with.

Your Personal Branding is now in session.

To your highest and best,

Matt ⦿

MATT WHITE

TABLE OF CONTENTS

Chapters one and two form the foundation of the S.U.I.T.S.™ model.

Personal branding is about understanding how to craft you and the business of being you. To do this, you will engage your highest intent for you, your personal brand, and take charge of your mental, emotional, and behavioural programming. Find out how to influence change that is channelled more than controlled and establish your statement of work, personal brand manifesto, and an intentional project plan for achieving your brand goal.

Having the authority and permission to create and execute a personal brand plan is the key to success. Through the neuroscience lens, you will explore a deeper understanding of positive chemistry to create energy in your system with the goal of higher integration and brand vitality. Personal branding is the application of self-actualisation. Within a bigger strategy, explore how to achieve the translation of your future vision into your present leader capacity.

Chapters three, four, five, six, and seven constitute the exponents of your S.U.I.T.S.™ model.

Achieving Iconic leadership status involves embracing your humanity and creating a tactical plan for achieving your goal. A tangible, valuable personal brand finds its roots in an integrated sensory framework, tying your body and mind together so that you can be powerfully present in your life. 'Paradox' and 'ambiguity' are resourceful partners in the creation of harmony in your work, relationships, and life.

Being an Iconic Leader requires you to have the ability to motivate, inspire, and encourage yourself and those you are leading. Thanks to your impact, your brand will go down in the annals of eternity. To achieve this, you will learn the fine art of connecting with your audience where and how it matters while you improve your asset base and connect with your stakeholders.

CHAPTER FIVE: IDENION

You are neither a victim of your personality nor a hostage of your future. In this chapter, you will find the keys to unlocking the potential in stereotypes and the ability to work with brand archetypes. Understanding how to package and position your value and recreating your interaction with your audience and yourself are central to this chapter.

CHAPTER SIX: TIMMULATION

The timing and quality of your interactions with your audience will lead your brand to the impact you want and establish your legacy. Timing is everything, and, as such, you will distil your value into timely, purposeful solutions which unlock strategic advantage and bring life.

CHAPTER SEVEN: SPLENDANCE

You are your story. Being able to tell your story with elegance and crafting the different climaxes is hard work that involves your resolution and efforts to build up tangible value. Your audience comprises characters who play specific roles, and the next thirty years in business will be all about the different stages of your efforts to connect authentically. Here, you will learn what it means to go the extra M.I.L.E.® and the art of keeping it R.E.A.L.®

MATT WHITE

PREFACE
BEFORE WE START
WHY PERSONAL BRANDING?

When you become an iconic brand, you instantly gain several advantages. They include promoting yourself, earning more money, and accomplishing whatever you set out to do.

> *"What happens when you are the right person in the right place at the right time?"*
>
> **– M. J. Nel –**

Being a celebrity does not give you Iconic Brand status. But it does mean that you are popular amongst a certain set of the world's population. Iconic Branding entails authentically owning and uniquely being you with integrity in your dealings.

A personal brand gives you credibility

People who own their identities are perceived as experts. Future employers, friends, prospects, and businesses see your name, and in our contemporary consumer culture, that translates into the view that you are credible and legitimate. It is clear that 'perceived credibility' influences the speed at which people develop trust and the basic factors they rely on when making purchasing decisions.

A personal brand gives you a platform

When you can prove through your brand that your unique opinion matters, mainstream and online media such as radio stations, TV shows, print media, and blogs seek to give you free 'time'. Content generation in our current consumer culture is about providing the user with unique insight, and these media establishments start every day with an empty page.

The value of having someone like you present a unique viewpoint is obvious. It grows their readership/listenership and supports your business ventures and personal goals.

A personal brand differentiates you

In business, the leadership of a company's CEO often directly influences its share price. Similarly, and more directly, the perceptions around you directly and indirectly affect your "share price" in your mind and in that of your audience. The idea that a single individual can affect the prosperity or failure of an entire organisation is probably the most relevant factor to understanding leadership's impact through self-mastery a.k.a. personal branding. Not only does your brand have personal value as it keeps you aligned to your true North, but it also uniquely positions you and provides the differentiation you require in the increasingly monochromatic world of good, highly qualified leaders.

A personal brand opens the floodgates of word-of-mouth

When you are known as the specialist in your field, uniquely differentiated and presenting all facets well, clients and future referrals will understand your genius and will know that they can count on you when they make contact. Your brand is therefore an autograph that they can experience in advance and a motivational driver, pushing you towards great achievements. Your signature is the key that will unlock the treasure they need to take their businesses to the next level.

A personal brand opens doors and attracts prospects

As I indicated earlier, personal branding is a matter of personal principles and business guidelines. When you make contact with new prospects and venture into other industries, you have the secret weapon of a well-crafted solution. The nuts and bolts of this book involve offering your audience an answer to its needs as you present your unique solution.

Clients who have previously experienced your work and can succinctly present what you're about are great allies who can open the doors that you're knocking on.

The S.U.I.T.S.™ Model metaphor

In the fashion world, where the newest trends are celebrated, I'm told that the proverbial black number is a must for every wardrobe. The S.U.I.T.S.™ model will take you through the creation of your black number, which will be appropriate for every function and will outlast any trend. Your SUIT will go through all the stages of tailoring: ideation, sketching, designing, pattern crafting, sampling, fabric selection, patenting and block engineering, the CMT (cut, make, and trim) process, fitting, tailoring, cataloguing, and showcasing.

The S.U.I.T.S.™ Model aims to provide you with tailor-made step-by-step assistance in the creation of the ultimate black number that will present you at your best and make you well known.

This could be a whole lot of fun

As I write this, I'm preparing to go on a trip to Barcelona and a cruise of the Western Mediterranean, an area with a rich history of magnanimous persons.

I'm going to the Med to take a break from everything: my social media, electronic communication, and set plans. I have just one focus in mind: taking this time to recharge and to review the multitude of conversations I have had since 1998. Many of these conversations have led to collaborations and businesses, projects and investments. As a result, I have exploited myself well.

My intention in taking this break is to have a very specific pause between two chapters, my previous life and the one that I'm going to lead, an intentional beginning and end.

So, the time in the Med will enable me to put together my ultimate self and put in place the permissions and decisions necessary to support this intent.

I have by no means experienced all the extensive human emotions to their fullest, but I know that this book and its many resources have unstuck me, released me, enabled me, and brought me joy and clarity many times. And some of those times, I've had a strong whiskey in hand.

You will find many things as you go through the pages: bullshit barometers, blame- and excuse-busters, frank questions, and compassionate viewpoints. All of them have been crafted with one thing in mind: enabling you to use your resources to achieve your ultimate intent.

Exponential acceleration

Many books offer leadership, brand, and business advise. Moreover, there's a staggering amount of self-help and self-improvement materials. This book is different. I have explored, vetted, experienced, put to the test, and applied everything in it to my own life. As such, I'm offering you a journey map.

Prepare yourself to have many 'aha' moments soon or in a matter of weeks.

Many of the questions may give you epiphanies on your way to work, in the shower before bed, or somewhere in between.

Putting together the different methodologies revolutionised my life. As a result, I have grown exponentially. Don't be surprised when you realise the answer to your questions was in front of you the whole time as you explore the different minds and constructs that S.U.I.T.S.™ captures.

For your performance

I have woven the fabric and patterns together so that you can show up SUITed.

In his book "Tools of Titans", Tim Ferriss asks, "What might you do to accomplish your 10-year goals in the next six months, if you had a gun against your head?" He goes on to say, "Do I expect you to take 10 seconds to ponder this and then magically accomplish 10 years' worth of dreams in the next few months? No, I don't. But I do expect that the question will productively break your mind, like a butterfly shattering a chrysalis to emerge with new capabilities".

The frameworks that you have impressed on yourself have led you to read this book. For that, I am grateful. However, they have failed to help you step up and recognise your ultimate self.

If questions unlock previously hidden abilities and remove blind spots, you hold in your hands the book of books, filled with mind-bending frameworks that you will treasure as you realize and recognize your potential.

Tailor your brand

The book is a journey filled with "Tailor your brand" sections, tools designed to help you achieve immediate and long-term returns. Massive changes will give rise to incisive, concise, conscious exercises that will give you the opportunity to achieve exponential results. The sections include frameworks, routines, reflections, models, techniques, supplements, and challenging questions.

Getting the most out of S.U.I.T.S.™

CREATE THE TIME

Each of us processes information and arrives at remarkable conclusions in a unique manner. Grant yourself opportunities by following the recommendations so that you may completely mature in your work.

INTELLIGENTLY REVIEW, REVERT, AND REWORK

Skipping a section in the book may be detrimental to the integrity of your work. I ask that you gloss over the sections that you are familiar with AND make a note to read them again. Many blind spots and performance-limiting gateways are often entrenched in unconscious competencies – the things you do on automatic pilot. Make room to read up on your area of expertise with new eyes.

THOUGHTS AND FEELINGS

Your thoughts about your thoughts about your feelings will take you meta – into the world of self-referential patterns. S.U.I.T.S.™ is designed to question the beliefs that you create around your thoughts and the resulting experiences. Hence, you can use it to craft your own best version of you and strive for your highest intent. Practice the art of questioning and answering yourself truthfully.

What is my intent with S.U.I.T.S.™?

1. My intent is for you to find yourself, create acceptance of yourself, and provide others with a way of enjoying you;
2. My intent is for you to access the resources you need to achieve your best version of success;
3. My intent is for you to have hope and create more compelling and inspiring current and future versions of you.

Layer upon layer

ARCHITECTURE

SUITS has two sections: Foundations and Exponentials. The Foundations section is there to provide you with the engineered plans for harmonising and securing the height of your achievements. The purpose of Exponentials is to create a virtual and physical matrix that is independent of and interdependent with the depth of your foundations and the ability to increase your reach and breadth exponentially.

AN ACT OF PASSION

Immersion in oneself and working on and in oneself can be serious business. The information in the book is nothing without your emotions and the connections that you forge with the content. It is incumbent on you to create the most resourceful way of engaging with SUITS, which will unlock the fun for you. This could include details such as where, how, and when you do your tailoring. It is important to have fun too. ⓦ

MATT WHITE

PREFACE

THE S.U.I.T.S. ™ MODEL

Are you ready?

As you start exploring and creating your brand, you will discover the entrance to the higher realms of personal development, which will lead towards excellence and ultimately provide you with an iconic expression of You.

> *"When I let go of what I am, I become what I might be".*
> **– Lao Tzu –**

And from there? I trust that you'll find the truth that I discovered for myself: that the sky is indeed not a limit but merely a point of view.

Personal branding is not a quick and simple fix; it is not even "natural". If it were quick and easy, more people would have achieved the milestones that you set for yourself. At one point, you may have said to yourself, "There must be more". Well, there is. And this book is challenging you to find out what it is.

Achieving excellence

In my training to compete in the 400 m hurdles at the Olympics, it was clear that, to master the endurance and technique I needed to be the ultimate athlete, I would have to apply serious effort. I will speak more about medals and the price of personal branding later. But, for now, I will point you to a caveat: In the application of such effort, less 'work' and more 'flow' are ideal because you are essentially tapping into your 'passion'. This gives you the energy to overcome the 'struggle' and stay focused while you have serious fun.1

In the fields of business and life, you require certain capabilities; unlearning, learning, and relearning the principles that govern the relevant discipline. Applying and practising these mechanics increase the likelihood of optimal transformation during your adventure.

Given the nature of the field and that which the title "personal branding" indicates, you will explore and map the alignment between you (personal) and business (branding). To achieve your intent, you will need to become a master of both. That includes your physical and mental worlds, which means that you'll be playing an "inner" game and an "outer" one.

During the process associated with the S.U.I.T.S.™ Model, if you accept the challenge, you will explore the structures that govern the basis of your thinking. You will kick off by probing the frames you set up that blindside you, limit your expression, and block your potential. The re-framing of these beliefs into resourceful structures is an outcome you can look forward to.

To deliver on my promise of freedom, I will share with you what I learnt in neuroscience, providing you with a workable model for reformulating the chemistry to create the energy you will need for sustainable change.

As you learn to think differently and explore the varied structures around your beliefs and values, your value offering will surpass your imagination. Your mind is continuously changing, and it governs the vitality of your being (mind-body-emotion). Consequently, you will engage other frames of reference, through which you will be able to track your progress.

To support you in the achievement of your ultimate intent, I have compiled a set of exercises using the META coaching model for META states, in which I am trained [2]. Moreover, I complement the exercises with third-party resource materials and technology.

The journey through S.U.I.T.S.™ is designed to allow you to run at your pace, in your time, for your needs. The only recommendation I have is that you commit and stay in the game.

In my final year of preparation for the Olympic Games, I suffered two injuries. One was physical. It entailed exhaustion and overtraining. The other, which was emotional, entailed divorce. Fortunately for me, over the prior three years of preparation, competition, planning, and dreaming,

> "The illiterate of the 21st century will not be those who cannot read and write, but those who cannot learn, unlearn, and relearn".
>
> – Alvin Toffler –

I realised I needed to make the shift for my entire self, not just for the sports enthusiast and adrenaline junkie that I was. This realisation, together with realignment and review, enabled me to gracefully bow out of a lifelong dream without being completely shattered.

Though I didn't achieve the goal I'd set for myself, I subsequently achieved a 'success' I hadn't foreseen. My commitment to the 'game' had gone through a metamorphosis. It was less about the medal at the Olympic Games and more about the medal 'of finishing the race', my race.

My ultimate intent was to be the best version of me – and I had the endurance to back it up.

Committing to your training

When you arrive at a point at which an exercise is indicated, I strongly suggest that you put the book down and do the exercise. Why? Because during my pre-hab and re-hab stages of training, it was often the little connective muscles and tissue fibres that caused me the big complications and trip-ups. Take the time to make yourself strong. In my experience, nothing is that urgent, not even the intimidating Inbox.

Every great and noble idea requires a period of sacred creation before it is ready for its cosmological birth.

Know that your personal brand will happen for you and that you are a worthy Brand. Understand that it may take a shorter or longer time to happen than you anticipate, but it will happen. In other words, you will be recognized for who you are, receive the recommendation and commendation you deserve, and have authentic interactions with those in whom you want to invest time.

The degree to which you're willing to let go of things, face the things that you've avoided, and commit to the things that are important to you as you consistently execute your plan is the degree to which you will experience success in your personal brand.

If you don't want to write in your book and would rather keep your exercises in one easy-to-access file in your cloud system for ease of reference, you can download worksheets at *http://www.mattwhiteinternational.com/shop/SUITS-worksheets/*. You will need the following code to download the complimentary file after registration: *SUITSTB*.

So here is your first exercise: Its goal is to mitigate your negative thought patterns and pin down your commitment, preparing you for your big bang.

Commit

My engineered brand will be active on or by: D D / M M / Y Y Y Y

There it is – you have a date.
NOW WE START.

✤ TAILOR YOUR BRAND: FIRST THINGS FIRST

PART 1 Open your diary. For the next eight weeks, set aside 60 minutes for every weekday and 90 minutes for every weekend day and allocate them to "BRAND <<your name>>".

PART 2 Now complete the following sentence by writing down the things that prevent you from achieving action and belief.

I DECLARE THAT I WILL NOT LET...

(here, you will list the things that intimidate you, keep you busy, neutralize your power, and slow you down; they can include past hurts, current struggles, and the internal conversations that put you down.) ... CONSUME ME.

_____

_____

_____

Signed on: D D / M M / Y Y Y Y

<<your full name>>   <<Signature>>

CONGRATULATIONS!
You have cleared your second hurdle.

Make a list

In order to support you in achieving your ultimate intent with your personal brand creation, use the following four tables to access the gateway into your untapped potential.

In the following table, use the first column to write a list of states (ways in which you do things) that powerfully describe you at your best – I have given you three examples; you can populate the rest of the rows. Complete the table with a minimum of 10 states. In the second column, complete the rows with words that describe your most resourceful capabilities and abilities. Give a minimum of 10 responses as you did in the first column.

THIS IS WHO I AM WHEN I AM AT MY BEST	WHEN I AM IN FLOW, I AM
Curious	Focused
Mindful	Flexible
Adventurous	Purposeful

▲ *Table One: My Best and Flow Table*

Now use new combinations of the words that you used in the table above to create new states for yourself in the table below - see my examples. Combine all the sets into new states.

I NOW HAVE PERMISSION TO BE
Curiously purposeful
Focused adventurer
Mindfully flexible

▲ *Table Two: Permission Table*

Use the table below to describe why it is important for you to have each of these states?

IT IS IMPORTANT FOR ME TO BE
Curiously purposeful: because I will be able to ask different questions
A focused adventurer: because I will be able to plan, start, and execute my branding journey
Mindfully flexible: because I'll be able to investigate analytically and won't be blindsided

▲ *Table Three: Importance Table*

In the last table in this section, write the descriptive state you will use in the different sections of your journey through this book using the table of contents as a guide. Add as many rows as you need.

THE SECTION OF S.U.I.T.S.™ I WANT TO USE IT IN	STATE
Chapter 1	Curiously purposeful: Because I will be able to ask different questions
Chapter 2	A focused adventurer: because I will be able to start planning and executing my branding journey
Chapter 3	Mindfully flexible: because I'll be able to investigate analytically and won't be blindsided

▲ *Table Four: Importance Table*

The art and soul of your personal brand

The DNA state and fabric composition of your thought life run at multiple levels in your thinking and feeling matrix. This matrix is a combination of your attitudes, beliefs, values, understandings, intuition, and knowledge. Your body uses its sensory systems to provide your mind with the information with which to create this matrix. [c]

Your internal information highway (the nervous system) has constant traffic which your visual, auditory, touch, taste, smell, balance, and movement systems provide. As a Master of thinking you create meaning (thoughts) about this information. The artist in you layers your thinking with 'higher' thoughts and creates higher meanings, and these become frameworks in your mind. Some of the higher frames become executive states and hold the power to be the elixir for your magick (an effort to make a change in one's life by using one's own personal energy) or the poison of your soul.

Use the table below to list your executive states, and rate them according to their degree of resourcefulness, where 0 is not helpful at all and 7 is extremely helpful. I have given you a few examples to get you started. Add as many rows as you need to comprehensively describe the extent of your resource centre.

The purpose of creating this list is not to craft a penultimate or exhaustive list. Rather, it is to get you thinking and to provide you with your first encounter with pattern spotting and pattern engineering. You can return to the table as often as you need to enrich and review the content so that you can unlearn, learn, and relearn it.

	0	1	2	3	4	5	6	7
I tend to see problems								
I expect people to reject me								
I tend to think optimistically								

▲ *Table Five: Executive States*

The list above will be the colour/texture through which you will experience your life. It is important to know this because, while such states control you, those whom you love, care for, are in business with, and are working towards another future with will have their own set.

The purpose of S.U.I.T.S.™ is to provide you with the best set of these executive states as you imbue it with flexibility and strength and learn how to 'package' your product for the best results for all the stakeholders.

Would it be valuable to have the ability to see your resourceful executive state in action?

What would the ability to adjust your executive state's strategy mean to you?

The manifestations of these executive states impact how you experience the world. They influence your relating, cognitive abilities, communication with others, and understanding of what is really going on.

Although paradox is part of your world (and, with great artistry, it can be relevant and resourceful), a paradoxical brand experience in which your mind and body and words and actions are out of sync can cause substantial distress and disease.

I think it prudent at this point in time to point out that you may come across an experience, definition, or challenge and find yourself thinking, "This isn't me". When that happens, go back to the executive state exercise, table five, write down what you would term your executive state, and ask yourself, "What is going on for me that makes this feel alien/weird/wrong?" Keep on asking the question about the new answer you get each time until the answer starts to loop – i.e. until you repeatedly get the same answer. At that point, reflect on what you have come to know about the matter and decide what to do with it.

Not every occasion calls for you to wear a suit, but every occasion in your life calls for you to be SUITed. The S.U.I.T.S.™ Model enables you to design and create multiple 'outfits', which will get you ready for all the adventures that you want (choose and desire). If I have my way, you'll be travelling light and will always be in style.

What is the link between the world and you? Have you considered how you create it? In my years as a personal brand strategist, employee engagement engineer, and executive coach, I have not found a Venn diagram that illustrates the conversation around purpose and profit with as much precision as the following one [3].

For clarity, I will refer to the following graphic as the Golden Circle diagram.

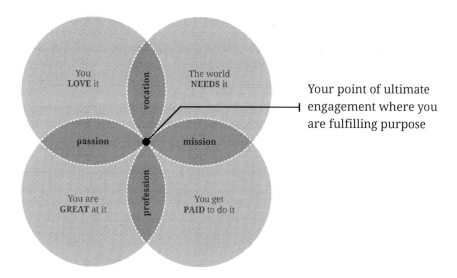

Your point of ultimate engagement where you are fulfilling purpose

▲ *Diagram One: The Golden Circle*

I have seen my clients use the above diagram in a variety of ways. Using it, I would like to take you through the plotting of the Golden Circle where the four areas overlap. For the purposes of this exercise, this area is the essence of your brand.

Before we pick up speed, I would like to offer you my definition of the four headings. Essentially, you have two sets of cousins. Each set is related at the root but different in application. The two sets meet at the beginning of your manifesto, your essence if you will.

Passion is a state, an intense desire that arouses enthusiasm, which can lead to strong emotions. It is therefore both energy (enthusiasm enacted) and meaning (the thoughts that you have about the matter) and normally serves an executive state or a value, something like "all human life is sacred". Your mission is that strongly felt ambition, the motivational driver, as a result of the meaning you give it. You have defined it and could define it as 'an important assignment', usually involving movement from one point to another.

Passion and mission are different in that you can achieve your mission (outer game) and finish dealing with the matter, whereas your passion is fuelled (the inner game) from one achievement to the next, and purpose is the golden thread that links them.

A profession is a particular occupation, whereas a vocation is a divine calling to service and can occur through a particular occupation. While a profession is focused on self-gain, a vocation is focused on benefitting others.

We will get back to the Golden Circle diagram in other chapters and enrich and understand it even more. The purpose of bringing the diagram to your attention at this point is to give you surety for which your brand will be applicable; we will be merging all the areas in the Golden Circle because that is what a considered brand does. Please complete the following exercise bearing the Golden Circle diagram in mind.

CREATING A PERSONAL BRAND MANIFEST

PART 1 Use the following table to describe the things you have done, the goals you have achieved, the activities you are part of that give you a sense of pride, and the feeling that swells your heart with the quiet satisfaction of pleasure. Use the right-hand column in the second part of this exercise.

▲ *Table Six: Sense of Pride Table*

In the table below, make a list of your talents and the things that are uniquely you: the qualities and features that you regard as being characteristic, inherently part of you.

▲ *Table Seven: Talent and Characteristics Table*

Make a list of the aspects of your profession and vocation from which you derive great satisfaction and fulfilment.

▲ *Table Eight: Satisfaction Table*

Using the space provided below, describe the activities and courses that you would like to add to your daily life to bring about more meaning for you and your brand experience.

▲ *Table Nine: Activities Table*

You are now ready to complete the first draft of your personal brand manifesto.

PART 2 To complete the manifesto, review tables six, seven, eight, and nine, using the right-hand column to mark the items in their order of importance (in your opinion): One indicates the most important item and seven the least important one among the items listed.

Personal Brand Manifest

Knowing that I am unique in *(the most imortant item from table seven)*:

I am committing to add *(the most imortant item from table nine)*:

To enhance my life in the fulfilment that I experience from *(the most imortant item from table eight)*:

So that I will experience the same feeling of enlightenment and delight when I manifest the characteristics of *(the most imortant item from table six)*:

CONGRATULATIONS!

You have created your first beacon towards finding and crafting your True North. Together, we will use and refine your personal brand manifesto with the goal of engineering the essence of what you're about and the great things you will achieve.

Do you know why?

In his book "Start with why" [4], Simon Sinek describes a model which is a simple yet powerful articulation of inspirational leadership. Your well-formed outcome will do just that. It will start with an understanding of "why" this is important [5]. During the journey of the S.U.I.T.S.™ Model, you will work in three parallel streams as you texture your Brand.

First will be your WHY: your reason for embarking on the work. Second will be your WHAT: your Personal Brand Strategy and Plan. And third will be the HOW: your Project Management and Change Plan. The three streams will constantly evolve and form the foundation of your work. 🌑

MATT WHITE

Branding and Project Management

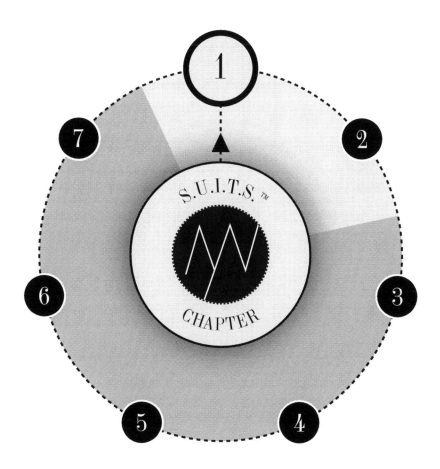

MATT WHITE

CHAPTER ONE

Much of the success you experience in life, as in business, is measured by the degree to which you successfully take others with you on the journey. I'm assuming that you're working through the S.U.I.T.S.™ model because you are ready for a richer life, are eager to embrace the benefits of your brand, and enjoy the rewards that come with owning your part in destiny.

The commitment that you have made is, in itself, change.

> *"No man is free who is not a master of himself"*.
> **– Epictetus –**

In support of your achievement of the new position, turnaround, and clarity, I suggest that you define change and how you will manage it. After all, you will need to facilitate the change which you want to achieve seeing as you're its root cause. Moreover, as you may have experienced, even your best intentions can result in catastrophe.

What is change management? It is the process through which change and development take place as identified and implemented within a system to achieve a desired outcome. Therefore, change management and project management are allies in bringing about the likelihood for success. What is success? Improving your brand experience and perception to achieve your goal.

You are many things: the founder, chairman, board, C-suite team, senior management, middle management, junior management, and employee to your Personal Brand. You, as much as everyone else, are a consumer of and stakeholder in your brand, and it is in the interests of all concerned that you find and subscribe to a change management methodology. Later in this chapter, I will present a change model for your consideration.

> *"Change is the only constant"*.
> **– Heraclitus of Ephesus –**

The change that you're bringing about for your Personal Brand, is a reaction to a specific problem and/ or an opportunity that you have earmar to address. Creating your personal brand will not be enough to bring about success. Change will come with hard work through the merger of the project management components.

So, you are now running two processes: One is focused on creating the brand and the other on achieving it. This requires discipline, a clear process, and the necessary tools.

As you start to introduce change in your Personal Brand, how people engage with you, the systems you are part of, where you fit in organisational structures, and the professional and social roles you fulfil and relate to will be impacted. The extent to which you can take people with you on the journey will determine how much success you enjoy.

As Personal Brand Change Master and Personal Brand Project Manager, you will require the application of your entire skill set, knowledge base, capabilities, and characteristics, as well as third-party tools and techniques to achieve your personal brand outcome (as you lead people and processes).

What do you think? Which tools are required for individuals to successfully adopt and transition into the new reality that you're creating? Are you aware that you are embarking on a lifelong journey of the integration of processes, initiation, planning, execution, monitoring, enhancing, controlling, and analysis?

The graphic below illustrates the process of project management and change impact.

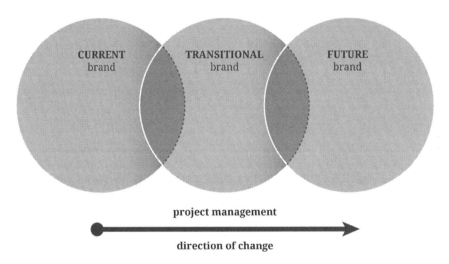

▲ *Diagram Two: Project Management and Change: Informed by PMBOK®*
Guide, Third Edition

As shown, the management process moves people from how things are today through the transition of what may come and into the desired future state.

Over the next few pages, you will create a basic project management structure to bring about the change you require for your brand. This part of the personal branding journey will evolve over the course of time and you will see many iterations. My suggestion is that you create a reference point that is both digital (something like Evernote™) and physical (a pin board at your desk and at home) to track your progress and offer you the opportunity to apply agility – making notes and changes as they become relevant. This will keep you accountable and energised as you maintain a full view of the scope and progress of your project.

A word of caution: Based on my experience, I advocate for momentum (consistency) over perfection at any time as the latter is an illusion. Change, by its very definition, is constant imperfection or constant perfection in motion – you get to choose.

While I'm offering you insight into a resource that will help you achieve your personal brand aspirations, take care not to get swamped and side-tracked by your need to fully understand, perfectly craft, or beautifully execute a portion of the project. Time is on your side, and you can do as many revisions as your heart desires of any piece of this body of work – but I urge you to stay with me, and keep moving.

Give yourself permission to enjoy the process and this program as you align yourself with the 'new'. What would happen if you had the permission to enjoy imperfection as an expression of perfection?

Over the next few pages, you will create several documents to which I will refer you throughout the process. The idea of starting these documents at this point is to give you a benchmark of your thinking and enable you to plan the things that you prioritise from here.

Amongst the many documents that you will constantly enrich are the following pieces of work, which constitute the foundation for the next phase: your Statement of Work, Project Charter, Business Case, and Budget.

Create a Statement of Work (SOW)

This is a 'formal' document in which you agree to whatever must get done. To be effective, the SOW must contain an appropriate level of detail. That will enable you to clearly determine what work is required, the time it will take to complete the work, the deliverables you're expecting, and what an acceptable standard would be.

Use the following table to populate the required areas.

General description of the Personal Brand Project, highlights of and reasons for the project, what stands to be gained. Answer the WHY.

What work is required

What must be delivered	By when

▲ Table Ten A, B, C: Statement of Work

Create a Project Charter

A Project Charter is a clarification of the objectives of your Personal Brand Project. The purpose of the statement is to set out detailed project objectives, goals, roles, and responsibilities and to identify key stakeholders.

From this point onwards, it is imperative that you consider the smart way to write [6]. The genius of George Doran has since 1981 influenced businesses around the globe with the mnemonic acronym, S.M.A.R.T.: Be Specific by providing details such as names, areas, places, measurements. Ensure that what you are committing to is Measurable – quantify and indicate how/what/where.

For tasks to be completed, someone needs to be accountable - who/what will be Assigned – specify. Is it Realistic? – state what can realistically be achieved, given available resources. How is time impacted – Time-related – specify when the result(s) can be achieved.

In conjunction with S.M.A.R.T., I recommend that you use RASCI [a]. It is a tool that enables you to identify roles and responsibilities during the change process. RASCI is an acronym. R stands for the one who is Responsible, owns the project/piece of work. A indicates Accountability, the one who must sign off/approve the work/piece of thinking before it can be effected. For a change project to be successful, you need Support; the S indicates the one who can provide you with resources or play a supporting role in the implementation or fast-tracking of the process. Understanding who needs to be Consulted – C – is a vital part of the information stream that develops capability and capacity. And the public relations piece concerns who needs to be Informed – I – this points to the people who need to be notified about results, progress, challenges, etc. but may not need to be consulted in the implementation of the project.

Should you have another method of gaining clarity on what you want to achieve, feel free to use it. Use the framework of the table below to create your Project Charter regarding what you think is required to capture the process of detailing the SoW and pushing it into action at present. To achieve your objectives (actions), support your goals (desires) with them (actions).

	DESCRIPTION	*R*	*A*	*S*	*C*	*I*
Objective 1						
Goal 1						
Goal 2						
Goal 3						
Objective 2						
Goal 1						
Goal 2						
Goal 3						

▲ *Table Eleven: Project charter*

In chapter three, I will support you by showing you how to create and break down the strategy and execution plan into a tactical plan that is measurable and manageable.

Write a Business Case

This is the part of the project where you review how ecological it is to pursue your goal of personal branding.

Do I agree that we all have brands? Yes.
Do I agree that we all need to review them? Yes. In fact, often.

This part of the work will bring you understanding regarding the time and relevance component of the project that you're embarking on. I like to define the Business Case during the early stages of personal brand development as it pulls and holds together the why, what, and how.

You have decided that it is worth working on a personal brand. To move forward powerfully, you need to answer the following four simple questions:

- What is your goal?
- What's stopping you from achieving the goal?
- How much change is necessary to achieve your goal?
- Are you certain this will solve the problem/address the opportunity?

In writing a Business Case for your Personal Brand, assess the following key components to provide evidence that supports your assumptions [7]:

- What is the business problem, or what opportunity do you want to maximise?
- What benefits would arise if you achieved the above?
- Are there any risks? What are you not saying or looking at that could potentially impact the success of your goal?
- Have you considered the costs, including investments, time, and other resources?
- What are the likely technical solutions that you could employ to achieve your goal?
- Now that you have considered all the aspects of the timescale, who will be impacted in terms of time when you achieve your brand goal, and what will be the impact?
- What will be the impact on your daily life and the operations of your work, relationships, and recreation?
- Do you have the capacity to deliver the project outcomes? Regarding the capabilities that you are short of, can you engage with appropriate service providers, and who would they be?

As you address each of the questions for your Business Case, describe the problem of the current situation and demonstrate the benefit of the new vision. Should you require more time from work, support from your relationships, or even financial investment, the Business Case will assist you in their procurement.

The three main reasons why projects do not succeed are poor project planning, a weak business case, and ineffective stakeholder involvement and support [d].

So, the risk of not devoting time to understanding your Business Case is failure.

However, you are empowered and are getting support regarding dealing with the above risks. You are therefore set up for greatness and have no excuse.

Engineer a Budget

The saying goes, "Everything has a price". One of the key outcomes of your brand goal could be increasing your wealth. To facilitate that, I will eventually show you how to create purpose in and to repurpose products and services which you can add to your income stream and well-being (together consummating wealth).

Newton's law formally states, "For every action, there is an equal and opposite reaction". I don't want to turn the branding project into a science and accounting exercise, but it does combine the two disciplines beautifully. The object of your branding project will be to increase your income (relational, monetary, career etc.), which is the action, so that you have additional resources to allocate to that which inspires and delights you, the reaction.

The purpose of the basic activity of engineering a Budget is to give you a reference point for the capital and other investments required and estimations of the expenses you may incur as you achieve your brand goal. Not everyone experiences the same level of comfort with numbers. So, if you are adequately comfortable, create an income and expense sheet in which you can itemise the income streams and define the expenses you foresee over the next twelve-month period. If you lack such comfort with numbers, now is a good time to learn an appropriate degree of affinity for the science and art of accounting.

There are many tools available from apps for your smart device to creating spreadsheet by hand on paper, in a ledger book, to using a database program as provided by the software companies for most personal computers.

Once you have decided which tool you'd like to use and have either downloaded or purchased the relevant material you can start with the foundation of making financial sense of your brand goals.

The components your 'spreadsheet' will need to include follow:

- An income section and an expenses section,
- Categories for subdividing the expenses and income,
- The indication of regularly recurring time increments (whether monthly, weekly, or quarterly), whatever makes sense for you in your context,
- An area that allows you to enter both anticipated and actual amounts,
- An area where you can total the income and total the expenses by time period.

Under your expense category, you may want to enter things such as web, which could contain monthly hosting fees, design, maintenance etc. You will also have physical product such as business cards, brochures, wardrobe etc. which you need to allocate in your expense sheet.

Whether you are comfortable with numbers or not, once you have engineered your budget, run it past a friend or a colleague so that they can provide you with an alternative viewpoint and input.

Foundational Success

The goal of your project stream is, therefore, to effectively support and deploy resources in a structured manner so that whatever needs to be done gets done. The project stream outlines activities that define and describe how you're going to move from point A to B. It also offers insight into what needs to change in your processes and structures.

In the change stream, you will find the steps necessary to help individuals in your world (whom the change that you're bringing about will impact) adapt to the new way and to assist with the successful transition from what was to what will be.

The Statement of Work, Project Charter, Business Case, and Budget exercise provided you with the guidelines for the project stream. From now on: this chapter will offer you support in the creation of your change management process. This points to the existence of three change cycles, namely, planning, managing, and reinforcing change [8].

Chapter two will start with my individual change components focused on you. As you have realised from using the RASCI model in your project plan, there is a need for communication, which is a key component of change. You facilitate successful change in Personal Branding by being your own biggest fan. The timeless methodology of coaching is something that you'll practice and experience as you lead yourself and others. As a side note, create a place where you can become comfortable with internal and external resistance to the change that you're creating. This is normal, and it will also help you fully evaluate your processes.

Changing how you change

Change starts with you. More specifically, it starts with your inner game: how you think about change.

This is a simple, elegant, inevitable fact.

As you make S.U.I.T.S.™ part of your everyday routine, you will realise that the secret to successful living corresponds directly to the extent to which you're comfortable with discomfort (change). In other words: action, reaction. Thank you, Isaac Newton.

Prosci founder, Jeff Hiatt, created ADKAR® [9], a change model that many of the organisations and individuals I work with have adopted. The acronym represents the five outcomes an individual must achieve for successful change: awareness, desire, knowledge, ability, and reinforcement.

Being part of change on a personal level implies that your thinking is changing and will continuously be challenged to change. Your change may be vigorous and ambiguous, and having structure to support you during this process will help you find your way back when you get lost.

I offer you this insight, not prescriptively, but to support and enable you.

You'll notice that, earlier in the book, we dealt with the A of ADKAR, Awareness. What are your reasons for change? This part of the process requires you to populate the change program with your reasons for change; it should assist you with crafting communication to the stakeholders of your personal brand. Communicating in advance to stakeholders regarding your reasons for change often has the unintended effect of eliciting support from areas that you did not expect to receive it. In addition, early communication flags stakeholders who may need the handholding approach.

D stands for the Desire to engage and participate in the change, and it applies to you and to those who may live a life of resistance (which the BORG will tell you is futile). Offering key stakeholders the chance to co-create your personal brand not only raises the desire factor for them, but it also keeps you motivated and energised as they offer you varying viewpoints.

The S.U.I.T.S.™ model will empower you with knowledge on the change you are creating. Jeff Hiatt's model is also about sharing the Knowledge (K) of how to change and the impact the change will have on your stakeholders; you need to clearly articulate and communicate this. Here, coaching becomes relevant for you with regard to your personal brand and for your key stakeholders.

Proficiency of change, even in technology, takes place on a timescale and seldom starts in perfection. It is often more of an improvement process. As you implement your personal brand, your Ability (A) to realise and implement the 'new' will increase to the level of required performance. You may want to call in the help of a coach and/or a mentor to practice the new gospel.

Reminding yourself through thought and behaviour that the old no longer is and that the new needs nurturing is the Reinforcement (R) you will need to engage in to ensure that change sticks. *

As you create your Change Communication using the model that you are most comfortable with, please review your Project Charter and Statement of Work and incorporate the thinking that you have already engaged in. They will both inform and assist you in your creation of messages that need to go out and will indicate who needs to be addressed. In crafting your message, consider the following: the purpose of the communication, the expectations of the recipient, the message, the context, what's next, and 'so what'.

Now reflect on your Project Charter and Statement of Work in the context of the Change Communication and decide on the best time for your communication and the best channel for the delivery of your message. In my experience, a cup of coffee between people having a face-to-face conversation often yields more than an email, *#justsaying*.

As you start to deploy your communication, keep track of your project schedule and review the speed at which you are communicating and implementing change. Being the agent of change and being on the receiving end of change are often different experiences.

When crafting and sending out the communication for change, you would do well to consider what the recipient is experiencing and to incorporate those considerations into your communiqué.

---

* *If you want to use the ADKAR Model, you can find a graph of it here: https://www.prosci.com/adkar/adkar-model. If you're more comfortable with another model for change and communication, use its framework and create the Change Communication.*

✂ *TAILOR YOUR BRAND: CREATING CHANGE*

Create your change model and match your ideal deployment time.

In summary - Chapter One

Accessing your highest intent for your personal brand is a process that involves taking charge of your mental, emotional, and behavioural programming.

You understand that crafting a personal brand is both about you and the business of being you.

Your ability to clearly articulate the program you would like to deploy for your brand can be indicative of the level to which you will experience its success.

In my opinion, change cannot be controlled, but it can be created and influenced, and the change program that you have created will support your ultimate goal.

Once you have created the Statement of Work and the personal brand manifesto, both the program and change management processes enable you to be intentional and to take a stance towards developing your personal brand.

What is in the next chapter

We will look at your current programs that you are running and establish the new frameworks for the ways in which you are and would like to be perceived:

- The blueprint of your chemical make-up;
- The environment and the events which shaped your decision-making;
- How to tap into your internal dialogue;
- Looking at the different viewpoints of being. Ⓜ

APPLIED NEUROSCIENCE

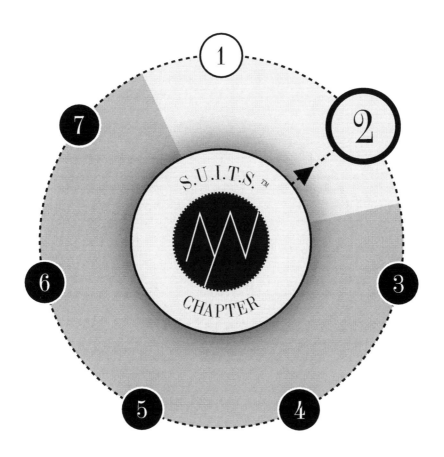

MATT WHITE

CHAPTER TWO

Re-think, re-imagine, re-be

It was quite by 'chance' that I found Tom Peters's book, "Re-imagine!" Admittedly, like Seth Godin, the author of "Purple Cow", I found the book "noisy, busy, brilliant, loud and insightful". It took me two years to finish reading it, and I revisit it often.

> *"The one with the sharper beak, the longer horn or the brighter feather has a better chance of surviving and procreating its kind".*
>
> **– Charles Darwin –**

Two things in Tom's work inspire me: He's not scared of writing from emotion and is quite happy to punch holes into egos.

So, this book and I with it are following suit.

The word 're-imagine' made me realise that there was an assumption in the title that I could imagine something and had, in fact, already engaged in doing so. However, I am not sure I was engaging my imaginative faculty – la la land scared me. This is a paradox, considering that I am a surrealist oil painter. However, through internal dialogue, I have been challenging myself to hope, dream, and imagine since 2003.

The part that still gets me is the 're-' part. It is simultaneously an energising war cry and a deliverance manifesto.

Can I claim to be free because I am using 're-'? Yes.

Am I free from being tantalised by opportunities and possibilities?
Not so much.

Do I still have to resist the devil of what I perceive to be both important and good for me side-tracking me? Every day.

'Decisioneering' my personal brand journey is a constant chess game for me in this disruptive age.

It was when I started my journey to qualify as an international Executive META Coach through the world of structured thinking that I found a way out of the adverse into complete liberation from the desperation that the statement, "There must be more," brought.

I have created the S.U.I.T.S.™ Model and am writing this book to offer you a way out of checkmate – an opportunity I wish I had much earlier in my life.

About the S.U.I.T.S.™ Model

The model is a framework that blends freedom/choice and structure.

It is up to you to blend the components to create the ultimate mix that suits you.

S.U.I.T.S.™, the mnemonic acronym (a pattern of letters that represents constructs that assist in remembering), is the title of the book and stands for the following: S – Strasion, U – Uniternity, I – Idenion, T – Timmulation, and S – Splendance.

Staying true to my personal brand as Neuro-Integrator, the model is systemic, non-sequential, interrelated, interdependent, and cohesive. If you have a need to interact with the model in a sequential manner, you'll find as much joy in it as someone who chooses not to.

The caveat to those who choose to engage with the solution in a non-sequential fashion is that they stand a chance of getting lost in the matrix and being assimilated by Agent Smith: "There's a difference between knowing the path and walking the path" (Morpheus, The Matrix).

The S.U.I.T.S.™ Model provides you with a path to walk down, and, along the way, you will learn about knowing.

Creating the experience you want

Use the following exercise as a think tank to formulate your expectations of yourself and of this book/model/program. Do you believe that "honesty is the best policy"? How would you 'do' being honest with yourself as you worked to craft your Personal Brand? Do you even have permission to be honest with yourself?

Once you have clarity on your permission, commission this piece of work. Consider using a journal to complete it as you may need a page to completely explore the richness of your answer to each question.

You can also use the downloadable file I created, which is here: *http://www.mattwhiteinternational.com/shop/SUITS-worksheets/*

WHEN YOU THINK ABOUT YOUR LIFE

a) How would you describe your contentment with the direction of your life?

b) What words would you use to describe yourself at your best?
(at least 20 words)

c) What words would you use to describe yourself at your worst?
(at least 20 words)

d) When others recognise and compliment you, what are the phrases and words
they use?

e) What exceptional and unusual expertise/knowledge/insight/capability do
you have?

f) What are the things that you believe in and that inspire you?

g) When you face hardship/challenges/obstacles, what do you do?
And then what do you do?

h) What activities do you engage in which have the most meaning for you?

i) List your dreams that are still unrealised.

j) Do you have secret silent passions for your life? What are they? What causes them to stay secret?

k) What role do you play in your broader family, community, country, and the world?

WHEN YOU THINK ABOUT YOUR WORK

l) Write the words that you would use to describe how you feel about your career.

m) Articulate the key goals you have set for yourself in your trade.

n) Think about your job goals and that which you want to achieve in your personal life: How would you describe them supporting each other?

o) What are you most proud of in your career?

p) List your biggest disappointments.

q) What knowledge/skill/capability are you currently developing?

r) What are the top three things you're expecting this program to give you?

▲ *Table Twelve A–R: Creating the Experience You Want*

✂ *TAILOR YOUR BRAND: CREATING YOUR PERCEPTION*

Take some time to review your statement of work, your personal brand project charter, and your change program in context of the work you have just done in Table Twelve, A–R.

- Enrich the documents with answers from this piece of work.
- Consider what you would like to add to the charter.
- Do you need to increase/decrease your scope of work?
- How are your timelines still relevant?
- Do you need to include or exclude certain people?
- What messages do you need to articulate differently?

Running your brand

The last decade has seen the influence of neuroscience in many spheres of business and in multiple industries. Perhaps the biggest breakthrough has been the application of neuroscience to understanding how to run one's mind and brain and the fact that they are different. As you create meaning about what you are experiencing, your chemistry changes. Being in charge of your thoughts is one thing; being in charge of your thoughts and being able to influence the resulting chemical changes in your body through the endocrine system is a whole different thing. This means that you're no longer a prisoner of your configuration of who you are and proves the ancient writings that say, "As a man thinks in his heart, so you will be" [10]. It appears that the ancients and the moderns agree: It is up to you.

As the body of collective knowledge and understanding of neuroscience increase alongside their impact, I feel privileged that I have obtained accreditation in the use of Dr. Ian Weinberg's neuroscience-based application. Dr. Weinberg is a practicing Neurosurgeon at the Linksfield Clinic in Johannesburg, South Africa. One of the key takeaways from working with his model is that, with neuroplasticity, we can all strive to truly be who we wish to be through consistency and motivation when we run our own brains and minds.

I'm introducing neuroscience into personal branding because your brand and your brain are foundationally linked. There's a plethora of information, toolkits, blueprints, and solutions to the secrets of success. In my opinion, true success is owning and running your own brain and mind and the resulting wonder.

With severe clarity, I remember receiving the first debrief regarding my online assessment of the Triangles Model ™. My then coach sat opposite me and prepared me for that which, unbeknownst to him, I didn't want to hear. The one thing that I thought I had managed to control and live my life away from was fear. It turned out that fear was the primary thing that motivated me and drove who I was at that time. I was shocked to my core to realise that.

I had spent a lifetime designing and living a life whose foundation was not fear – and all I ended up doing was feeding my fear.

With a mixture of gratefulness and unease, I undertook to eradicate fear – and I can now tell you in hindsight that that was a typical fear-based response: making a vow to disavow fear. Why was it typical? Because I was afraid.

Over the next four years, I lived and created the S.U.I.T.S.™ Model, which I put to pen. This model now helps me to get out of my head and inhabit my life, further proof that I am similar to Tom Peters (I also write with emotion). I have tremendous compassion for my fellow human beings in our perfect imperfection and deep yet incomplete understanding of the nuanced complexities we individually face.

I trust that the S.U.I.T.S.™ Model will be a gateway to freedom and an anchor of sanity for you as it has been for me.

Black and white and shades of grey

There was a time when the world believed that all swans where white. This belief was prevalent because there was no empirical proof to indicate otherwise. And then the world discovered Australia and its black swans.

In his book, "The Black Swan", Nassim Nicholas Taleb (2007) writes about the biases we form and how we confirm them using evidence we source by looking through a specific lens. This catastrophically closes our minds to alternatives and possibilities, ultimately blinding us to other truths.

This is the result of an unresourceful state where you fail to achieve your best intentions as a bimetric system (that which you are by nature and that which you have become due to nurture).

Your heritage (nature/DNA, genetics, and family bloodline) is a set of dependencies over which you had no control. The other factor that influenced your chemical make-up concerns how you were raised (nurture) from the moment your parents knew that they were expecting a child. The convergence of these two spheres (nature and nurture) ultimately created your foundational bias and determined your configuration (how you view the world and subsequently interact with it).

You will connect with and experience the world (your inner and outer game) through your set of lenses, which was formed and still is being formed by your nature and nurture components. Moreover, your perception of the world and the meaning you create for yourself will influence your health and well-being in body and in mind.

Having said that, I want you to understand that there is another way, a way out of the old life and into the new one, the one you want. It's a way to find black swans, and I am evidence of it.

There is significant proof that you can rewire your history, recode your genetics, and access your ultimate intent for life. It is also implied that you have the choice to walk away and, like the penguins from Madagascar, say, "This never happened" [11].

Dr. Weinberg's deep and enormous contribution through his Triangles Model™ quantifies the chemistry of wellness, performance, and leadership [12]. In the next few pages I will take you through the pieces of the chemistry that you should understand so that you can incorporate it in your scope of work and craft your personal brand with precision.

With the knowledge that you have about nature and nurture and the proof that neuroscience brings, I trust that you believe that who you are is a matter of choice, not just of disposition. The statement that goes, "Well, this is just who I am," no longer holds you captive. What does this new insight give you? *

How is your relationship with energy?

For the purpose of illustration and to design your ultimate brand as you achieve your highest intent, you can utelise the following four power zones from which to derive your energy: emotional, mental, physical, and spiritual.

I liken the four zones to four cylinders in the engine of a car. They are independent and interdependent. This means that when one slacks, the other pulls, and there is constant movement and shifting. This essentially results in forward motion. The petrol and the oil in the engine simulate purpose, meaning, and motivation. The decision toward action can be likened to the spark which the ignition activates.

The illustration implies that if one of these areas in your life is ill-nourished, the others will need to make up for the shortfall, putting undue pressure on the system and inevitably leading to malfunction and breakdown.

The contextual reality is that if all your cylinders are not firing, you're not performing at your best.

✂ *TAILOR YOUR BRAND: ENERGY ZONE AMPLIFICATION*

PART 1 Draw four circles on a page and name each circle to indicate that it is a different source of energy.

PART 2 Now write the words associated with your activities and describe the behaviours (yours) that contribute to or detract from the energy source. Also consider the actions that are missing.

PART 3 Next to the activities and behaviours that positively contribute, make a '+' sign, and next to those that detract, make a '-' sign.

PART 4 Now, next to each word/behaviour, write the amount of time that you invest in or spend on it.

Calculate the number of positive and negative hours in each circle and write the answers below: one answer for the positive (investment) hours and one for the negative (expense) hours.

- -

* *To accelerate your growth and your understanding of your configuration, you can do your own online assessment. Contact my desk at: pne@mattwhite.international for more information about the way forward.*

With your mathematical mind, calculate:
- The shortfall or excess of energy in each zone,
- The percentages of each circle as they relate to one another.

PART 5 From this perspective, enrich your working documents (SoW, Brand Charter, Change Model) with the answers from this four-circle exercise.

Consider what you would like to add to or take away from the circles, and adapt your documents.

Does this influence the scope of work? How does this influence the timelines? Is it sustainable for you to make these changes? What is the context of these changes (with whom, when, where)? Can you effect these changes? *

Are you playing cloak and dagger in smoke and mirrors?

Abraham Maslow's Hierarchy of Human Motivation [13] presents a ladder that theoretically moves you from physiological needs, through safety needs, belonging and love needs, esteem needs, cognitive needs, and aesthetic needs, to self-actualisation so that you may achieve transcendence.

The theory presupposes that you could finish (completely meet the needs of) a level and move on to the next.

In practice, as with the four energy zones, these constructs are in constant flux.

By way of illustration, take Bob, a successful executive in a financial institution responsible for marketing and communications.

In his vocation, he transcends himself to serve others by creating innovative banking products that support the masses and boost their financial well-being. Yet his belonging and love needs remain unmet, resulting in a pending divorce. This is where Bob and you are similar – you play the presence of well-being when, in reality, you have to manage the complexity of your life and its unfulfilled needs.

---

* *If you lack vitality (the state of being alive and active) and want to access the energy that the mitochondria (the powerhouses of your body's cells) produce for increased physical performance, maintaining your mental capacities, and good sexual relations, search for the Pharmanex Vitality AgeLOC product. You can also contact my desk at: vitality@mattwhite.international for further information.*

Changing gears

Your body runs multiple processes at the same time – *#notnews*.

Have you considered that your processes are manumatic, a class of automotive transmission that allows you to conveniently control gear selection? For the most part, automatic transmission in vehicles allows some control of gear selection, making downhill braking possible and minimising overdrive in gears during towing.

In its capacity as an ecosystem, your body is similar, minimising wear and tear and increasing performance at will. With S.U.I.T.S.™, your META processes (thinking about your thoughts) enhance your state of equilibrium with features such as 'manual mode' - selecting available gears by shifting up and down using the steering wheel-mounted paddle shifters of your modified shift lever. You can achieve this through your new awareness of your executive states.

The executive process that aids your body's health and well-being is called homeostasis; it is the body's ability and tendency to move towards a relatively stable equilibrium of interdependent elements as it relates to the four energy zones (in illustrative terms) but especially as required by physiological processes. Allostasis is the executive process through which your body responds to stressors to regain homeostasis, allowing you access to the state of genius you can flourish in.

This means that, without your assistance in the creation of positive meaning, your body strides towards a state of balance rather than a state that allows flourishing [b], maintaining a non-satisfying delusional reality.

Homeostasis and allostasis is intrinsically programmed into every molecule of your being. You will specifically find the control centre in the hypothalamus. Inherently, your brain triggers certain behaviours to enable your chemistry to realign you, for instance, lighting up a cigarette, having a cup of coffee, or eating chocolate. Your endocrine system will behave strangely and often trigger behaviours that have addictive implications in the effort to regain balance, and this is where the previous three behaviours become a challenge. These triggered behaviours could be anchored in any of your needs in Maslow's ladder of motivation.

What am I saying? Notwithstanding your best intent, you could naïvely anchor behaviour from within a 'deficiency need' that is not supportive of a 'being need' – a higher motivation.

To mitigate the risk of unresourceful behaviours for legitimate needs in your personal brand, do the following exercise.

✂ *TAILOR YOUR BRAND: MOTIVATION LADDER*

PART 1 Create for yourself a ladder of the hierarchy of motivation – see the ladder below this exercise. Next to, or within each level, record the areas of your life, passions, goals, and needs that remain unfulfilled as they relate to each level.

PART 2 Use the information from your four circles as a cross-reference for the enhancement of your energy zones.

PART 3 Mark the areas on the energy zones and the motivation ladder that are priorities for you in achieving your goals for your personal brand.

PART 4 With these new insights, enrich your working documents (SoW, Brand Charter, Change Model). Turn the words and constructs that you have marked as priorities in achieving homoeostasis (towards transcendence) into actions and goals as you add them to your working documents. *

TRANSCENDENCE

SELF-ACTUALISATION

AESTHETIC NEEDS

COGNITIVE NEEDS

ESTEEM NEEDS

BELONGING & LOVE NEEDS

SAFETY NEEDS

PHYSIOLOGICAL NEEDS

▲ *Diagram Four: Motivation Ladder; A. Maslow.*

* *If you would like a more scientific quantification of what motivates you, contact my desk at* <u>*motivation@mattwhite.international*</u> *and we will be in touch with details.*

Do thinking and think doing

My friend and mentor, Robert Smale, created the Translation Point™ model. This model visually represents the translation of vision into strategy, informing the tactics that should be deployed. The result is task definition: defining what needs to get done for the achievement of the vision. The tasks have owners, and an execution plan supports them.

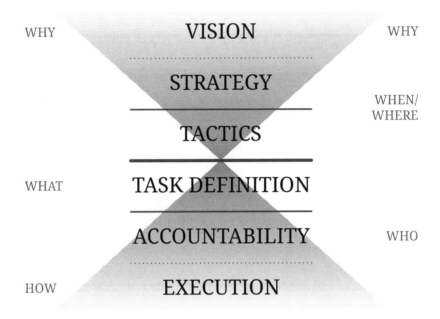

▲ *Diagram Three: R. Smale, Translation Point ™ Model.*

This illustration succinctly places your working documents in a screenshot. With this view, you can use your visual acuity to place all the artefacts that you have worked on so far and interrogate what may be missing.

In his work, The Reactive Scope Model – a new model that integrates homeostasis, allostasis, and stress [14] – Michael Romero refers to the variance of influences that mediate homoeostasis as a result of stress (a state of mental and or emotional strain and or tension resulting from adverse or abnormally demanding circumstances). The purpose of providing you with the Translation Point model is to moderate your sense of feeling overwhelmed if you're experiencing it at this point, thereby limiting negative stress.

Michael goes on to say in his work that predictive homoeostasis (relating to seasonal/environmental change), reactive homoeostasis (unpredictable change), homeostatic overload (concentrations/levels of change below the predictive homeostasis levels), and homeostatic failure (disease) exist.

When you combine predictive and responsive change, you have what one could term 'normal' change. The parts that you should take cognisance of in your change model are the overload and failure components.

What this means for you, working on your personal brand, is that change comes whether you're creating it or not, and influences you and those in your audience in a variety of ways.

Essentially, you are the cause of stress in your life and those of others. How do you relate to this statement?

Being aware of the general wear and tear of change, the gradual loss that a system/person endures to counteract an unpredictable impetus, will go a long way towards managing successful change and your transportation of your audience towards your desired destination.

TAILOR YOUR BRAND: WORKING DOCUMENTS – ENHANCEMENTS

Review your translation point and allocate to your working documents environmental influences such as previous stressors that people may have experienced. These could include past social changes and life experiences that you are aware of which could influence the success of your personal brand creation and the positioning of your audience in your life.

Furthermore, consider the social and life experience changes that will result in the new brand.

- Consider who is at risk of losing track and may need a roadmap.
- Is there a trend amongst your audience members and stakeholders?
- What resource can you implement in your strategy to assist yourself and others with 'normal' change?
- Are there any systems/processes/people suffering from overload or failure, and what impact could they have on your personal brand creation and positioning?
- What makes it appropriate for you to act in support of your ultimate goal as you review the environment/context in which you're creating your personal brand?

The chemistry of branding - applied neuroscience in personal branding

The following section deals with the dynamic relationship between adrenaline, dopamine, and serotonin.

What is so frightening about fear?

At the heart of fear – if fear has a heart - is the experience of an unpleasant emotion. Where does it come from? From your belief that someone or something is dangerous, likely to you cause pain or discomfort, and could be a threat to your homeostasis – life and life as you know it.

Now that doesn't sound so bad.

However, in practice, the possibility of experiencing an unpleasant emotion wreaks havoc far and wide.

You know that you create meaning around your thoughts. So, you sit in the command and control centre as captain and, therefore, as the creator and sustainer of fear.

Earlier, I referred to stress – a state of mental and or emotional strain and or tension (the inner game – what goes on in your head and heart) – resulting from adverse or abnormally demanding circumstances (the outer game – what goes on in your life).

You are familiar with homoeostasis and its various shapes and forms. Consider this wild idea – how you think about that which places abnormal demands on your capabilities, capacity, and abilities is merely an opportunity to grow. And somehow you respond with fear, panic, anger, and rage. Blend a measure of tiredness and hunger into this concoction and what you have is a delicious cocktail of depression, anxiety, and an emotional outburst or meltdown. This cocktail is best served chilled with a nasty twist of zest. Does it sound familiar?

Consider the following words: "Do you know anybody who really does not want to feel in charge of his or her life? I don't. After two decades working as a psychotherapist, I cannot remember a single depressive who didn't want to have more control and power over his or her life. Actually, it was each person's sense of not being in control, that he or she was out of control and powerless, that triggered the depression and sense of helplessness" [15] (Dr L. Michael Hall).

It seems that lack of control could lead to depression. What if depression was only a state of hopelessness (not having the resources one needed) and helplessness (being stuck without a solution to a challenge)?

> *"Anticipation of pain leads to fear, and fear amplifies pain. Expectation of relief from pain increases the opioids in the brain, makes the hurting stop. How you react to pain determines how much pain you actually feel".*
>
> **– The Bearded Man, Orphan X, Gregg Hurwitz –**

In the next few pages, I will dive into the depths of your transmitters and the messages which will provide you with the necessary tools to generate an alternative. Alternatively, they could help you manage unpleasant experiences with more resourcefulness.

Magnum Opus: Your most important and best work yet

Adrenaline is the body's activator. It gets you to do things and is exceptional at enabling you to climb ten-foot walls. Adrenaline is released in response to purpose, anticipation, anxiety, exercise, and/or fear; so it's not entirely a bad thing. The amygdala plays a key role in the how and when of manufacturing adrenaline. Your thoughts and the production of adrenaline are the basis for the so-called fight-or-flight reaction.

Adrenaline is a natural stimulant, and its biological name is epinephrine. It is produced in the adrenal glands and carried in the bloodstream, which affects the autonomous nervous system. This, in turn, controls functions such as the heart rate, the dilation of the pupils, and the secretion of sweat and saliva.

A feeling of sudden intense fear (fright) causes the brain to send signals to the adrenal glands – which are among the endocrine glands that produce a variety of hormones, including adrenaline and the steroids, aldosterone and cortisol. The renal glands start pumping large amounts of adrenaline into the bloodstream, which increases the heart and breathing rate in preparation for the ensuing action.

The amygdala is a small, almond-shaped mass of nuclei. You have two – one in each lobe in the brain. They function to control fear responses and emotions, your motivations, and your actions.

They also play a role in the functioning of your memory as they interact with the hippocampus (the elongated ridges located on the floor of each ventricle of the brain) and the temporal lobe (the parts of the brain lying beneath the temples) to establish 'event' memories.

The amygdalae form part of the limbic system, and their size correlates with aggressive behaviour – this is a case where 'size does matter' is completely true. The bigger they are, the more aggressive your behaviour. [12]

The amygdalae receive input from all senses (smell, taste, sight, hearing, touch, movement, balance etc.) as well as the emotional input from your thoughts. Since they play an important role in emotional learning, the highway from the emotional centres of the brain is a major source of input.

The emotional metropolises are the:

- The **septal nuclei** play a role in reward and reinforcement along with the nucleus accumbens. [i]
- The **orbitofrontal cortex** is a prefrontal cortex region which is involved in the cognitive processing of decision-making. It is defined as the part of the prefrontal cortex that receives projections from the magnocellular, medial nucleus of the mediodorsal thalamus, and is thought to represent emotion and reward in decision making. [j]
- The **ventral striatum** is a critical component of the motor and reward systems. Practically, the striatum coordinates multiple aspects of cognition, including motor- and action-planning, decision-making, motivation, reinforcement, and reward perception. [k]
- The **anterior cingulate cortex** resembles a "collar" surrounding the frontal part of the corpus callosum. It is involved in certain higher-level functions, such as reward anticipation, decision-making, impulse control, and emotion. [l]
- The **insular cortex** (also insula and insular lobe – insulae) are believed to be involved in consciousness and play a role in diverse functions usually linked to emotion or the regulation of the body's homeostasis. These functions include perception, motor control, self-awareness, cognitive functioning, and interpersonal experience. [m]

The amygdalae receive olfactory information (the sense of smell) from the olfactory bulb – a neural structure in the forebrain that is involved in the action and capacity of smell or the sense of smell.

Auditory, visual, and somatosensory information (information about sensations such as pressure, warmth, pain, and movement) come from the temporal and anterior (front) cingulate (a curved bundle of nerve fibres) cortices (the outer layer of the cerebrum), which offer insight to the brain and give you the opportunity to create additional layers of meaning.

That is a mouthful. So now what? The purpose of this section on adrenaline and the amygdalae is to give you an understanding of how intricately you are wired for sensory input and the effect it has on your energy levels and actions.

If you consider this section in conjunction with homoeostasis and allostasis, together with the four energy zones (spiritual, physical, emotional, and mental), I trust that you will see how it is possible to create an addiction/aversion out of any interaction/activity due to the energy that you get from it and the meaning that you create around it.

✿ *TAILOR YOUR BRAND: TAMING THE ADRENALINE BEAST*

Answer this: what immediate change can you bring about to significantly improve your use of adrenaline?

In the context of the section on adrenaline, consider your four energy zones. Replace the activities in the four zones with activities that align with more resourceful actions towards your ultimate intent - adapt the activities to correlate to the amount of energy you receive from each of the zones and must invest. You may need to moderate some other factors so that the four energy zones are maximally resourceful.

Recalculate and calibrate the scores in each of the zones as you did the first time you reviewed the four energy zones, and reflect on the impact of these changes on the working documents: the SOW, Brand Charter, and Change Model. Adapt them accordingly.

Would there be value in creating a list of fears that you carried so that you could bust them using the facts in your working documents and the exercises you have done thus far? If so, go blast them!

Have all the fears that intimidate you been addressed in the work you have done up to this point? If some are outstanding, add them to your working documents and address them with solutions.

✿ *TAILOR YOUR BRAND: MAXIMISING FULFILMENT*

- Create a scorecard with three areas: an area that entails your professional activities (how you apply yourself e.g. work, studies, philanthropy etc.), one that describes your relationships (with yourself and others), and one that focuses on fun (leisure and relaxation).
- Give each section a name that best describes it (for you).
- Under each section, list the constructs that you must have a handle on. For example, your professional activities section could include things like the level of success, responsibility, conflict, stress, support, etc. Other constructs to bare in mind are esteem, pleasure, stability, and empathy.
- Create a scoring system that doesn't have a median (for instance, 0 to 7 or 1 to 4) and for which the lower end of the scoring scale indicates zero satisfaction and the higher end indicates complete satisfaction. Score your current satisfaction with each of the constructs and each of the sections and tally the totals.

> • With the insight that the scores give you,
>   - How can you resourcefully harness the power of each of the sections in your fulfilment scorecard?
>   - What activities can you add to your project and brand charter?
>   - What is the impact on your change model?
>   - Is what you are creating for yourself as a personal brand still realistic?
>   - How much do you want this new personal brand given all the work you've done thus far?

One of the key things about the kind of work you're doing at the moment is knowing that you are 'safe' and in charge. I would be interested in knowing how you rate your safety as you are currently experiencing it.

If you need more 'safety', what can you do to make it possible? When you are safe, what do you and your brand experience?

Drugs, Sex and Rock and Roll!

The purpose of the section that described adrenaline and its sources was to enable you to create a strategy that intimately resonated with your highest intent and debunked the myths that had bound you over the course of your life.

Fulfilment plays a huge part in your performance as you achieve that which you set out to do; experiencing hope, happiness, joy, and pleasure is key to being in excellent health.

The Nucleus Accumbens plays a role in the brain's loyalty program, your reward and recognition system – and you thought that R&R was a corporate invention for customer and employee engagement. When you do anything which you consider rewarding (like eating food, drinking coffee or alcohol, having sex, taking drugs) your dopamine neurons (nervous system cells designed for electrical and chemical transmission of signals) are activated.

These neurons communicate with the nucleus accumbens when activated, and this results in an increase in the dopamine levels on the nucleus accumbens's highway in the brain (it is called the mesolimbic pathway).

When you experience success and pleasure adequately (e.g. during a rewarding experience), the pathway starts to resemble peak traffic.

The only difference is that there is constant flow. Thus, it is no wonder that pleasure plays an important role in the reward system. Increased dopamine traffic helps to regulate the adrenaline in your system, bringing it to a more resourceful state.

But it is not all about blue skies. The nucleus accumbens also plays a role during your reinforced learning. Not only is it connected to the processes of resourcefulness, but it also concerns how you deal with fear, aggression, learning, impulsivity, etc. and the rewards that you obtain by dealing with things the way you do.

It is possible that when you experience a reward from an adrenaline high resulting from a fear response, your wires get crossed and your brain processes fear as a reward. You need to hear that your brain cannot distinguish between good and evil. That is your job. That is why you have a mind: because sometimes your brain doesn't know better.

Figuring out how your loyalty program works is more intricate than it seems. The following exercise will help you define and reprogramme your R&R system if need be.

> *"Health is a state of complete mental, social and physical well-being – and not merely the absence of disease or infirmity".*
>
> **– Preamble; World Health Constitution, 1946 –**

TAILOR YOUR BRAND: INCREASE YOUR DOPAMINE

What Went Well for Me Today, is a journaling technique that positive psychology guru, Martin E.P. Seligman [16], created.

It is an exercise that takes on the form of a gratitude journal. I am presenting an adaptation of the technique here for your personal brand.

There is sufficient scientific proof that dopamine is also released in the anticipation of pleasure and success, not just when one experiences them. The purpose of the What Went Well exercise is to find and define both the anticipation of sources of pleasure and success as well as the actual experiences thereof so as to increase your dopamine levels.

The trigger could be the experience of something on the day in question or the anticipation that something will happen in the days to come.

Experiment with listing entries relating to each of the energy zones, i.e., what you experience mentally, physically, emotionally, and spiritually. These could range from cuddling the cat to being invited to a talk show. As you get in touch with your daily life, the compounding effect of positivity and resilience will have both short-term and long-term benefits.

You need to reflect on your day. Create entries (at least three; even better, you could incorporate one from each energy zone) about the things that you are grateful for before you go to bed every night for twenty-one days.

- The first part of the "what went well" exercise is about making your journal entry – naming the specific event;
- The second part entails adding a sentence as to why you think it happened that way;
- Third, articulate what it means to you;
- Fourth, make a note on how you can have more of this good thing in the future, and decide if you want to include it in your living artefacts;
- Fifth, conclude your entries with a note on why you believe it is important for you.

Writing these entries by hand has proven to involve more grit (scientifically) than typing them up or doing a voice recording. It offers you the opportunity to own your realisations.

Dancing into happiness

When you are healthy and able to manage your thoughts and, specifically, your ability to bounce back from sadness, anger, and anxiety, you have a reservoir of happiness.

The skills involved in enjoying positive emotions are different from those involved in dealing with negative emotions.

In my experience working with leaders over the years, they are exceptional at dealing with negative emotions and struggle with creating, acknowledging, celebrating, and fostering positive emotions.

Being happy creates serotonin, and sufficient serotonin makes you happy. Your body creates it naturally through the biochemical conversion of tryptophan, a component of proteins, using tryptophan hydroxylase, a chemical reactor. When the two parties come together to tango, they form serotonin, a.k.a. 5-hydroxyltryptamine (5-HT) which is commonly referred to as a happiness neurotransmitter.

Essentially, serotonin is found throughout your body and not just in your brain. The majority of the body's serotonin, between 80-90% of it, can be found in your intestines, and the balance is present in your blood platelets and the central nervous system.

Interestingly, serotonin cannot cross the blood-brain barrier. Therefore, the brain must produce the serotonin that it uses. For this reason, being happy in your thought-life is an important state of mind.

What do serotonin and its production have to do with your brand? The mere fact that your thoughts and the associated meanings create the required serotonin, your happiness drug, enables you to bounce back after events associated with negative or unresourceful experiences such as sadness, anger, and anxiety.

At this point, you should understand that your thoughts regarding their meanings influence how you regulate your adrenaline and the amount of dopamine that you have access to; they also enable you to manufacture the key ingredient of joy.

People follow brands that engage, create meaning, and help them achieve their goals on multiple levels. Brands do this by inspiring them through shared interests and values as they create customs that are oriented towards a higher purpose and impact.

If a brand fails to produce happiness, it will fail to inspire its audience and subsequently miss the mark.

As happiness is critical to your experience of joy in life, serotonin is believed to play a key role in the nervous system and the general function of the body. Studies have found links between serotonin and bone metabolism, breast milk production, liver regeneration, and cell division.

✂ *TAILOR YOUR BRAND: HEALTH CHECK*

Do the following health check on the package that your personal brand comes in. On a scale of 0–3, where 0 is unsatisfactory and 3 is completely satisfactory, how would you rate the following:

* Your bowel function and movements?
* Your appetite reduction during a meal?
* Your ability to elicit happiness?
* The extent to which anxiety negatively influences you?
* How quickly your blood platelets clot when you're wounded?
* Your libido and sexual functions?

Literature on the association between depression and serotonin has been published widely, and there is still uncertainty in certain spheres regarding whether decreased levels of serotonin contribute to depression or depression causes a decrease in serotonin levels. Medical research is ongiong. What are your findings as this matter relates to you?

✂ *TAILOR YOUR BRAND: SEROTONIN SAMBA*

PART 1 When you look at the results of the above scorecard, how do you think you should change your personal brand charter, the change model, and your income and expense document to accommodate the creation of the appropriate amount of serotonin?

PART 2 Review your four energy zones and ask the following question: Where could a lower serotonin level create risk? With this insight, adapt the personal brand charter.

PART 3 Create a cheat sheet for yourself that will enable the appropriate manufacturing of serotonin. Use the following guidelines to populate it, providing you with a framework for a dynamic routine: *

- The number of hours that you're exposed to natural bright light;
- The type, variety, and duration of the exercise you choose to do;
- A healthy daily diet that consists of protein, fats, and carbohydrates whilst limiting sugar and syrups;
- An adequate amount of rest, sleep, leisure, and hydration.

Trauma and the nervous system

I spoke about creating 'safety' earlier in this chapter. As S.U.I.T.S.™ integrates neuroscience into personal branding, I would like to take a moment to explain why safety is important by offering you insight into trauma.

---

* *Do you need to supplement? Supplementation with vitamins and minerals, as with other things, has its place. In my experimentation with different multivitamins and minerals (and I have done a lot of that), I found that the ultimate multivitamin for sports nutrition, weight management, and general health and well-being was Double X.*

If you want power-packed support for a healthy heart, brain, eyes, skin, bones, and immune system, find the Nutrilite product, Double X. Alternatively, get in touch with my desk at <u>doublex@mattwhite.international</u> *should you require assistance.*

As a professional, I spend an appropriate amount of time investigating the past and its influence on my current experience of life. I require time to reprogramme the past in order to support my homeostasis and achieve my future.

When memories limit your future by showing up in your present, you should investigate the possibility that trauma has something to do with that. Trauma is complicated, and its influence on you experiencing safety is vast. It is a phenomenon that is challenging to understand. You are a complex and wonderful human being, and how you deal with trauma is very different from how I deal with it. This section is less about diagnosing trauma and more about understanding the effects it has on how you create your personal brand.

Trauma is best understood through its effects on the brain and nervous system. It can be about a specific event or a chain of events (that may be related or not), and there is nothing unique about having trauma in your life – we all experience it. So what is it? It is simply your experience of an event in which your ability to integrate the emotional piece, the meaning you create about the event and how you feel about it, is overwhelmed. The memory of the event is 'fragmented' during the filing process and, as a result, it impacts your wellness and performance. Trauma often takes place when your safety is compromised, and it may be linked to your survival.

The brain stimulates your defensive actions when information received from your senses activates it. Earlier in this chapter, I mentioned that fear and threats did not have to be real (a physical manifestation in other words) for your brain and body to react or for you to create meaning around the associated incident.

Your body's response to a traumatic event or series of events can often continue long after the event – abuse, war, extreme training, etc. – trapping your body's processes and keeping the activation of your arousal hormones in place. This means that you're now stuck in 'fight, flight, or freeze' mode. Because your body is exceptional at reestablishing homoeostasis, you may no longer even be aware of your behaviour. Overexposure to the trauma may have turned it into a new norm.

For all the negative publicity that 'fight or flight' has received, it is a wonderful mechanism that keeps you alive and what it would term 'safe'. What happens when you can't escape or protect yourself from an apparent threatening experience? It is likely that your self-defence mechanism in your brain becomes muddled. A possible casualty could be your ability to create and sustain healthy boundaries and manage time effectively.

Consider the filing of traumatic memories as a three-part information byte. Part one is a non-verbal component such as a body sensation, picture, smell, or sound; part two is a thinking (cognitive) part; and part three is a 'feeling'/META part (thoughts about your feelings about your thoughts about the experience).

Imagine them being filed separately from each other and remaining unrelated in your brain and nervous system. The result could include a variety of destructive behaviours [17]. For instance, when you smell a specific fragrance, you can behave in a completely irrational way as your behaviour is informed by a totally unrelated experience and 'you don't know why' you don't like the smell. Some other tell-tale signs could be dysregulated feelings of being overwhelmed, inappropriate defensive responses, hypervigilance, and out-of-sync sense-based emotions. It all depends on which file the amygdala accesses when another situation unrelated to the original trauma triggers a safety response.

✿ TAILOR YOUR BRAND: CREATING A SAFE ZONE

Fight or flight is a very good way to stay safe, but it is not a plan for a thriving life.

Consider the history of your life. You could perhaps use a timeline that extends over decades to help you reflect.

Ask yourself if any unresolved traumatic events are keeping you from being your best. Curiously and tentatively investigate how some of your current behaviours are linked to those past events - you may even challenge behaviours that you historically thought were resourceful or that you were complimented on.

If you presume that every behaviour has a positive intent [18], how could you recreate these old behaviours to make them positive behaviours towards your genius self and achieve your best future state. Do you need to delete the program altogether and install a new one?

Allow yourself to wonder what it would feel like if you had to feel completely safe. Would it have value for you? And if you were completely safe, what would be different about your behaviour?

How would this sense of safety, together with your new behaviour, influence your brand charter?

> • Are there any behaviours or activities in your energy zone exercise that need to be re-evaluated?
> • Have any of your motivational factors changed?
> • Is your statement of work still relevant?
> • Does your budget need to be adapted to accommodate new behaviours and activities?
> • How does this new awareness impact your change model?

Being the leader you need

Self-mastery and personal leadership are key to successful personal branding. Through this work, I trust you've realised that both capabilities are seldom complete or finished. A further dimension of personal branding, which is never complete, entails people's perceptions of your brand, your audience members' minds, trials, and priorities and the oscillation of the context in their space (environment). You will find that your brand is in a constantly changing territory.

The Harvard Business Review published an article on "The Incomplete Leader" [19] that discussed possibilities around leadership and the challenge that it presented. The answer for leaders such as yourself entail primarily embracing their humanness and recognizing that failure and success are part of how they manifest their set of strengths and weaknesses. It is another example of imperfect perfection at work.

Secondly, it deals with embracing the organisational needs within which you operate in the context of the following four areas:

- Sense-making – interpreting developments in the business environment, making sense of what is going on;
- Relating – building trusting relationships as you may have experienced what relationships without trust achieve;
- Visioning – communicating a compelling image of the future. Here, clarity regarding what future and what communication were paramount;
- Inventing – coming up with new ways of doing things, where the meaning of new was key.

Merging your powers (capabilities and abilities) and energy (motivation, vitality, and drive) with those of people who complement you in your areas of deficiency is the fundamental premise of unleashing self-leadership and the promotion of your brand.

🎗 TAILOR YOUR BRAND: MOVING FROM LEADING SELF TO LEADING SELF AND OTHERS

Neuroplasticity is your brain's ability to restructure itself by forming new neural connections throughout its lifetime to adjust activities in response to new situations or to changes in its environment. It is a technique widely used in a variety of areas and industries and specifically in the medical field as a way in which to assist patients that suffered loss or the use of a specific body function.

I use neuroplasticity in personal branding to help people rewire their brains through a set of conversations and frameworks to reclaim their minds - how they think about themselves, their resources, the world, others, and time and how they subsequently interact with these constructs [20]. Although I only introduce the concept of neuroplasticity here, you formerly were and still are being exposed to the practice throughout your opera omnia.

Brands help us to choose what we truly value and guide us in the choices we make towards the experiences we want. Think about how you would like to lead yourself, how you would want to be shown the way, and the direction in which you would like all parts of yourself to be guided.

Now, as chieftain, someone who has special abilities and qualities, create your HERO brand: the brand that has godlike prowess and beneficience.

As you honour your HERO brand – which is courageous and able – consider the following:

- What traits (ways of being) are you required to polish up on, mediate, and downplay to successfully lead yourself and inspire others to follow you?
- What part of your personal brand leadership is currently timeless and what part is aspirational?
- What steps and stages would you progress through to build elegant leadership and achieve your ultimate brand experience?
- If engaged leadership has effective interruption and well-timed intrusion as traits, what other character traits would you like to add to your personal brand to achieve these two factors successfully in your environment?

Take time to review your thus-far-created living artefacts and enhance and enrich the documents as appropriate. *

A bag full of seed - taking stock

What have you been keeping yourself busy with up to this point in S.U.I.T.S.™? If I may make a suggestion, the model has guided you to create fertile ground for the flowering, bearing fruit and procreation of your personal brand, a.k.a. seeding.

---

* *You can get a technical view of how you currently organise your motivational drivers and leadership preferences by getting in contact with my desk at ic@mattwhite.international. We will be in touch with details.*

You have also been busy with so much more.

You have viewed yourself as though you were a Crystallographer, applying the science and investigating the homogeneous entity (sum of related parts) that you are. You may have noticed that your brand has natural geometry (a regular form with symmetrically arranged planes), is symmetrical in places, ordered, (even if you don't understand it), and three-dimensional (because you are multifaceted). How you cluster atoms and molecules (your processes and innate capabilities) is unique, another expression of seeding.

You have also practiced the ability to arrange your players (capabilities) to engage for the ultimate tournament, life, by creating positions so that ranking players (resources) are ready for your matches throughout your season, yet a further expression of seeding.

You will continue with seeding throughout the following chapters as you engage in 'peer-to-peer file sharing', evaluate the flow of your liquidity, and review your thinking – still seeding.

❧ TAILOR YOUR BRAND: SOWING FOR SUCCESS

I'm interested in knowing how your internal dialogue is going. Use the following set of questions to guide your thinking so that you can enhance your living artefacts.

- What sense of self-awareness do you have? Do you have a conscientious handle on your character, feelings, motives, and desires?
- Regarding yourself, have you come to accept what you previously couldn't?
- In the conversations that you have with yourself, which parts of your personal brand can't you accept any longer? What is your action plan regarding them?
- To what extent have you grown in your self-esteem?
- How would you rate your conviction regarding your own worth and abilities?
- What are the areas that need investment for greater self-esteem?
- Do you respect yourself like you would a mentor?
- Do you need to change how you engage in self-respect?
- What area of your self-confidence still needs your attention?
- In which areas do you trust yourself and in which areas do you not?

> • How has your attitude (the way in which you think, feel, and behave) towards yourself changed? What sensory-based proof (what you hear yourself say, what you see yourself do) are others able to give to show that you have changed in these areas?
>
> • Do you have your permission to stand in awe of yourself? To what extent are you celebrating You?

In summary – Chapter Two

You made the acquaintance of S.U.I.T.S.™:
S – Strasion, U – Uniternity, I – Idenion, T – Timmulation, and S – Splendance.

You reviewed your permission structure in the same way that you think about your life and work and created action points to activate a plan for achieving your intent.

Through a preliminary view of neuroscience, you gained an understanding of the basics of your positive chemistry cycle and explored ways in which to enhance your chemical structure and function.

By exploring where your energy is generated and how you can create more resourceful activities, you are moving towards higher integration and vitality.

As you investigated your motivational ladder and explored areas of life that may have required your attention for fulfilment, you were enabled to stabilise and maximise your strategy for a purpose.

All the documents you are working with (the Statement of Work, Brand Charter, Change Program, and Budget) are condensed into a one-page view through the translation point.

Trauma can inhibit your best. By dealing with the pieces that are still active in your system, you are achieving new levels of happiness and peace.

You have started a new journey to lead yourself and others.

What is in the next chapter?

- Together we will investigate your raison d'être (reason for being).
- You will create the strategy document for your personal brand.
- As part of the strategy, you will create an execution plan with milestones using the project charter we created in chapter one.
- You will explore the S.U.I.T.S.™ personal brand framework. ⊗

STRASION

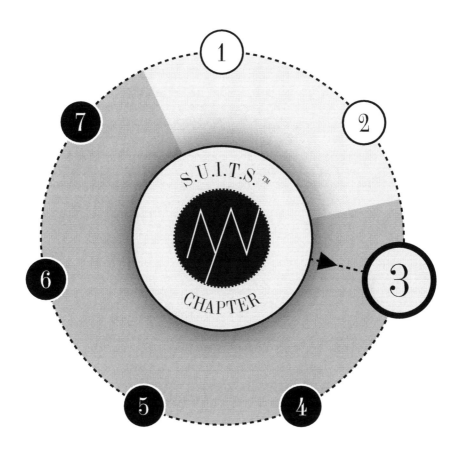

MATT WHITE

CHAPTER THREE

Integrator: Getting it to work

> *"People say nothing is impossible – but I do nothing every day".*
>
> **– Winnie the Pooh –**

My personal brand positions me as a 'neuro-integrator'. I integrate the brain's chemistry and the META processes (the meaning we create and allocate through thoughts and feelings) in conversation, using frameworks to achieve the ultimate objectives of business and people.

From the work that you have done thus far and your experience of integrating your brain, mind, and body into a brand expression, you may understand the critical role that integration plays in iconic leadership. And leadership is the cornerstone of your future, my future, our future.

Our future demands that we transform, inspire and motivate, engage with vision, and manage the delivery of what we promise whilst we coach ourselves and others towards a higher level of achievement.

Many experience this statement as the foundation for disruption.

Fact: There are times when disruptive behaviour is a rudimentary requirement.

This statement raises eyebrows in that higher, better, faster, bigger, cheaper, cleaner, etc. mean that the current state of affairs is not ideal. I have learned that the '-er' at the end of these words indicates a state of change. It is up to me to determine whether that's better or worse and then to decide what to do (or not), depending on how I use the energy from my chemistry on that which has changed. And that is all there is. My subscription to the illusion of the ideal has expired, and, in its place, I have embraced the gift of presence – very mindful of me. ;)

Iconic leadership is the extent to which you're able to elegantly blend the required components at different points in time as your future demands to achieve the temporary state of the ideal mutation.

Why temporary? Because change is constant. What defines the required blend of components? The outcome that you want. How will time be decided? By the construct you create based on your sensory disease.

As an integrator, I have created five new portmanteaus. A portmanteau is a word made up of words that are connected by a theme, for example, 'guesstimate', which is made up of 'guess' and 'estimate'. Apparently, the first time a portmanteau was used was in the book by Lewis Carroll (1871), "Through the looking glass", where Humpty Dumpty explained to Alice, "Well, 'slithy' means 'lithe and slimy' and 'mimsy' is 'flimsy and miserable'".

The new word combines the sounds and meanings of the old and refers to a new state. It is pretty much what you are doing with your personal brand: taking the old, creating the new, establishing an altogether fresh world that is related to the well-used one - interrelated and independent.

This is the reason why I am a neuro-integrator; I get to be a Personal Brand Alchemist, a catalyst, supporting you as the inventor of your story as you move from imagination to reality.

Sensory-Informed Brand Framework

Your ability to sense is a physiological capacity which you obtain from an 'organ' or a system that provides you with data from which you create perception (bringing into awareness).

There are many fields concerned with the study of sensory information, including neuroscience, cognitive psychology, and the philosophy of perception. All the data gathered from your senses is transported through your nervous system from the areas that have been allocated and dedicated to that specific sense.

Most people are familiar with the five senses: sight, smell, touch, taste, and hearing [21].

A portion of the population would argue that they have a sixth sense – intuition. They are not wrong about having a sixth sense; their list is just short of a few others and they have managed to mix apples and pears (emotions and feelings – more about this later). The reality is that researchers would argue that you have 21 senses.

As a neuro-integrator, I have selected the data sources for your personal brand that make the most sense (pun intended) for this work. As you work through the sensory-informed brand framework, you're welcome to include that which will enhance your personal signature.

To the five I have already mentioned, which you know well, add the following for brand amplification. I have also included some examples of where, why, or how the sense is important for your personal brand integration. Bearing in mind that your personal brand is a perception in the mind of your audience, how you physically 'show up' directly impacts the current or future perception of your brand and, therefore, impacts your product and service experience:

Vestibular sense:
The sense of movement and balance in terms of direction and acceleration changes and, of course, gravity awareness;
➡ *because it can inform your ability to create, purpose, and repurpose energy.*

Proprioceptive sense:

Your ability to tell where your body parts are in relation to other body parts and where your body is in relation to 'space';

▶ *because it can enable your understanding and processing of space and relation of constructs as well as the ability to pinpoint emotions and yourself in a territory such as a map of the underground.*

Pressure sense:

Your awareness of applying and experiencing pressure that is different from touch;

▶ *because it can provide you with the capacity to distinguish the urgent from the important.*

Stretch sense:

There are receptors in the lungs, bladder, stomach, and gastrointestinal tract. These receptors sense the dilation of blood vessels and are also involved in headaches;

▶ *because it supports self-regulation.*

Itch sense:

A distinctly different sensor system from other touch-related senses;

▶ *because it can reinforce your ability to deal with frustration.*

Hunger sense:

The sense that detects when it is time to have something to eat;

▶ *as it assists you with 'hanger' and its possible consequences.*

Thirst:

The sense that enables you to monitor hydration levels throughout your body;

▶ *because it drives your survival and abundance constructs.*

Tension:

The sensors are in your muscles and enable you to monitor muscle tension;

▶ *because you become aware of your needs and those of others.*

Thermoception:

Your ability to sense heat and cold, internally (in your body) and externally (from outside your body);

▶ *because of how it enables your awareness of your body's inflammatory response.*

Nociception a.k.a. pain:
Initially, you may think that this is an overload of other senses. But there are three unique systems responsible for communicating pain; there are cutaneous (skin), somatic (muscles, bones and joints), and visceral (body organs) receptors.

➧ *because of how you communicate and interact in a state of exertion.*

Chemo sense:
These receptors trigger the medulla in the brain, which enables you to detect hormones and drugs in your blood. They are also involved in your vomiting reflex;

➧ *for understanding and managing different states that manifest as a result of trauma and strain.*

Magnetoception:
This is how you detect magnetic fields, and it is very useful in providing you with a sense of direction;

➧ *because it supports your sense of purpose.*

Time sense:
This sense has been contested because humans do not have a singular mechanism that allows our perception of time, yet some of us can 'intuitively' tell the time;

➧ *for knowing how you process being 'in-time' and move'through-time'.*

The Sensory Informed Personal Brand framework uses sensory input as a model and forms part of the backbone for S.U.I.T.S.™. I have found that it is the most common frame of reference for the integration of what you are about and how you connect with the business of being.

What is most valuable about the sensory-based framework is that you integrate the processes that you are already running (feeling, thinking, doing) with information received from your body as you engage in the activity of alchemy (transformation) with the new systems that you draw from.

As you grow, from a young age, you learn how to process sensory information and create the framework that support your focusing of attention on particular sensations while ignoring others. So the brand framework also serves as a challenge to open up the data streams, which could support you in mitigating the frustrations and difficulties that you have experienced in business and relationships.

In the work that I do with children, the integration of senses is fundamental, and there is sufficient proof that adult behavioural challenges can be pinned to sensory integration during a person's formative years.

I have also realised that the integration of senses without facilitating the creation of meaning and the ability to affect change within an individual's system leaves him or her short of the iconic leadership requirement of the future. (If you have children and are concerned for their sensory development, see *www.kasi.world* for ways in which we can support you.)

Creating a system that provides feedback and can mirror information for what it is and being able to use the information to adapt in an agile way is another benefit of the sensory-based personal brand framework that you will experience.

Consider the following list of challenges that you may experience as a result of deficient sensory integration to gain an understanding of how important it is to have your information channels open. The channels are there to support you, but you may have chosen to ignore them. Create a scoring system such as 0 to 7, where the lower end of the scoring scale indicates 'never true' and the higher end indicates 'always true'. Score your current experience of each of the constructs.

- You appear to be disorganised most of the time.
- You have difficulty transitioning between activities and environments.
- It seems that you are easily distracted and have an inability to pay attention to tasks.
- You are unduly unaware of or under-reactive to touch, movement, sights, or sounds.
- You may be impulsive or lack self-control.
- You struggle to calm yourself once you are riled.
- Performing tasks with both hands is strenuous for you.
- Your activity levels are exceptionally high or low.
- You have difficulty figuring out technology.
- You grapple with body awareness and coordination, which causes you to appear awkward.
- You find that your social skills lack dimension and texture, and this shows up in team environments or aspects of change within the business.
- What insight do the above scores give you?
- How else does this currently show up in your personal brand expression?

✻ *TAILOR YOUR BRAND: SENSORY INTEGRATION FOR ENHANCED INTELLIGENCE*

PART 1 With a review of the senses, you can now consider your four energy zones and examine the activities you have in each zone. Earlier, I asked which of the activities you participated in (though these could have included great activities such as exercise or meditation) were getting in the way of your being your ultimate best.

> • What senses would you like to develop further by increasing activities that stimulate them to benefit your personal brand?
> • What do you believe this augmentation would bring about for your personal brand?
> • Do you have new insights on your less resourceful behaviours viewed through the lens of sensory integration?
> • What understanding do you now have of your personal brand and the importance of the mind-body loop?

PART 2 With the adaption of your four energy zones, what enhancements do you need to make to your living artefacts?

PART 3 Using the following table, which you will also find in the complimentary online file, start your personal brand framework by populating the table with the highest values of relevant senses. You're welcome to give more than one value for each sense, and you can use words or sentences to fully illustrate your meaning. Later in the work, you will be required to prioritise your sensory systems as well as your highest value for each system in the Strasion section – chapter three.

There are senses that could overlap with one another in your activities. When you create the activities in your energy zones, ensure that the primary focus of each activity is the corresponding sense as in example I in the table.

Sensory System	Your Highest Value	Energy Zone and Activities to Actualise the Sense	Goal
Sight			
Smell			
Touch			
Taste			
Hearing			
Vestibular			
Proprioceptive	Courage	Physical: Go for Muay Thai lessons once a week Mental: Do primal movement exercises every second day as part of my warm up in the gym Spiritual: Go on a silent retreat every quarter with the first one in Spring. Emotional: Do meditation on my lawn daily at the end of my work day before I connect with my family	Physical: To stand my ground Mental: To connect with my body Spiritual: To engage with the Spirit Emotional: To be mindful of what is going on for me

Sensory System	Your Highest Value	Energy Zone and Activities to Actualise the Sense	Goal
Pressure			
Stretch			
Itch			
Hunger			
Thirst			
Tension			
Thermoceptive			
Nociceptive			
Chemoceptive			
Magnetoceptive			
Time			

▲ Table Thirteen: Sensory-Informed Personal Brand Framework

Business Brand Strategy

When I facilitate Brand and Business strategic sessions in what is perceived as a linear process, the experience is completely the opposite. I pay attention to what the company has learned in the past, the markets in which the product/brand/business idea worked, the enhancements that are necessary for it to continue working in current markets, and what the competitors are busy with.

With this understanding, I start exploring with the team why it finds communication (marketing/sales/advertising) necessary, what problems it will solve for the customer, which business objective it is trying to achieve, and which big thing needs to get done.

This opens up the conversation about how the brand's identity and personality will manifest in campaigns through specific behaviours, what the consumer will take from it, and what story the business will tell through the brand in order to become a tale that the consumer will want to be part of.

Having checked that the brand guideline supports the business intent, we discuss how success will be measured in the context of the key target audience. Ultimately, we clarify the expected experience and quantify how the audience's desires and needs will be met. The golden thread that holds the business strategy accountable to the brand strategy is the essence of the vision that the leaders have for the business and checking that this is actually important to the audience.

The next set of chapters is about the personal brand framework that translates strategy through the translation point into action.

Plan it - Strasion;

Your first portmanteau is Strasion; it is the unison of strategy and vision.

I define Strasion as "the creation of a thought, concept, formed by the imagination that is inspiring and the art of universally planning and directing the operations and movements of the thought, concept, to a manifested state."

> *"The more you read, the more things you will know. The more that you learn, the more places you will go".*
>
> **– Dr Seuss –**

I have participated in many boardroom vision-setting sessions. They all have in common the apparent thought that setting goals is the way to solve the current experience of the future. It fascinates me that somehow creating the future using a set of goals has become standard practice and that crystal-balling, dreaming about the future, has become a warm and fluffy practice.

I find this quite captivating simply because having this type of vision, daring to dream, is so much larger than setting obtainable goals.

Another observation I have made about these boardroom sessions is that when the executives in the room are not clear about their visions for their lives, they simply cannot create inspirational stories to attract the organisations' energy for the businesses over the following three decades. This also contributes to the shortfall in achieving a Massive Transformative Purpose [e].

Strasion is about getting clear on your vision and crafting the strategy to support that vision for your personal brand. If you want to create sales, design a twelve-month initiative. If you want to build a business or achieve a goal over three years, craft channels to support your intent. If it is a brand you want, then set aside the time – decades.

Vision in the Context of Iconic Leadership

In the preface to this book, in Table Four, you created a state to use during Strasion. You are now going to use it. What was that state? Can you fully access it now? Is it still the most resourceful state for you to use? Is it everything that you have become aware of? How do you rate your iconic leadership ability?

Brand provides relationships through which people interact and vision provides the direction that the brand and its people are going in. Strategy sets priorities, and goals are markers by which achievement is measured. The current state of anything is an impoverished place in which to look for motivation – in my opinion. Hence, Strasion. Purpose, on the other hand, is quite a compelling state of inspiration and abounds with motivational energy. That is the atom we need to split.

> *"The true sign of intelligence is not knowledge but imagination".*
> **– Albert Einstein –**

My work in the business field, where I am a trusted advisor to my clients, often takes me through several methodologies as I explore what organisations and their people are going through. In preparation for your Iconic Leadership, I have done the same with you. I have laid out a pathway of multiple processes. Leadership, at its core, is a disruptive force. Apart from being proactive (solving problems, anticipating needs, and not being satisfied with the status quo) iconic leaders must prove that there is a reason for others to tell stories about them as they follow willingly.

This means that your purpose must be both compelling and convincing, demonstrating the integrity with which you're pursuing it as a worthy tribute that the bards of your time will want to sing about. The richer the picture, the more ways to explore it, the more compelling. As an effective Iconic Leader, a mere mortal, you must learn to slay the fire-breathing serpent, face the titans of your time,

> *"I will take the Ring", he said, "though I do not know the way".*
>
> **– Frodo, J. R. R. Tolkien, The Fellowship of the Ring –**

and save those in distress – not only for the benefit of others, but also for the fulfilment of your potential.

What quest are you called to that only you can achieve, Frodo?

Here's an important question: What is your reason for being here? And equally important is this one: What do you want to do about it?

Votre raison d'être – your reason for being

In the preface of this book, you created a personal brand manifesto.

- Was the thinking that you applied in the creation of the manifesto big, audacious, and transformative?
- Was there enough energy there to unlock your purpose?
- In the context of how you understand eternity, will the personal brand manifesto you created matter?
- Does it actualise your life ambition?

IS YOUR BEGINNING YOUR END?

I remember phoning my functional fitness coach to explain to him why I was not coming to the session I had scheduled for that day; he invited me for coffee instead.

After he sat me down and closed the door to his office, he proceeded to challenge me concerning what was going on with my training. During the conversation, it came to light that I had achieved the goals I had set out to achieve. His infamous words to me were, "Your goals were too small." That was why I lacked motivation to train on that day.

He continued with: "What do you need to do to become alive again? What is big enough for you to throw all of your effort behind it?"

As may be the case for you, physical training and exertion were an escape and an addiction for me - a way to hide from my pain and to deal with my disappointment in a constructive manner. He had found me out.

Although he was referring to my fitness goals, the impact his questions had on the actualisation of my life ambition was beyond his comprehension.

I knew full well what I needed to do in that moment, and it scared me.

I had to raise my dreams and hopes from the dead and end the reign of Leviathan in my life. I questioned my capacity, my vocation, and ultimately my purpose. I had to scrape courage together, step into destiny, and allow myself to be disappointed and vulnerable. That conversation, amongst many subsequent ones, was a cataclysmic event in my life.

My life as I knew it, would never be the same. The conversation touched every part of my existence and permeated into every relationship, aspiration, goal, and enterprise that I got involved in. It still does today.

The purpose of the story is to embed the requirement for coaching conversations about the things that really matter. If you're unable to answer with a vision the questions of the first paragraph of this section, sit down with your coach and have the conversation.

If you're unwilling to answer these questions, now is a good time to close the book: "This is your last chance. After this, there is no turning back. You take the blue pill – the story ends, you wake up in your bed and believe whatever you want to believe. You take the red pill – you stay in Wonderland and I show you how deep the rabbit-hole goes" (Morpheus, The Matrix, 1999).

Purpose in action

Having created your personal brand manifesto (vision), page 34 of this book, you have essentially locked down a short concise statement of your future and indicated where you would like to be. This purpose that you penned and birthed out of your deep desires and aspirations addresses the timeless expression of your quest to accomplish your vision. Your personal brand charter is proof that it exists – your reason for being.

> ### *INVICTUS*
>
> *Out of the night that covers me,*
> *Black as the pit from pole to pole,*
> *I thank whatever gods may be*
> *For my unconquerable soul.*
>
> *In the fell clutch of circumstance*
> *I have not winced nor cried aloud.*
> *Under the bludgeonings of chance*
> *My head is bloody, but unbowed.*
>
> *Beyond this place of wrath and tears*
> *Looms but the Horror of the shade,*
> *And yet the menace of the years*
> *Finds and shall find me unafraid.*
>
> *It matters not how strait the gate,*
> *How charged with punishments*
> *the scroll,*
> *I am the master of my fate,*
> *I am the captain of my soul.*
>
> **– William Ernest Henley,**
> **1849–1903 –**

The sum of all the documents you created and are reviewing is the declaration of your existence and independence. Happy Independence Day – now get to work!

✂ TAILOR YOUR BRAND: THE VALUE OF PRINCIPLES

The work that remains outstanding is our completion of the principles/values that will guide and manifest your passion and distinctive core. So, defining your core begs a set of questions.

You can create a scorecard of your values and principles using the following questions to guide you:

> • What do you stand for?
> • What ideologies (systems of ideals and ideas) ground you?
> • What is non-negotiable for you?

Once you have concluded the work on your values and principles, enhance your living documents with the appropriate amendments. *

Magic tricks

True luxury is simplicity – clarity. What is the purpose of introducing luxury as part of the experience of your personal brand? A luxurious brand is a desirable item of great cost, which is difficult to obtain – the presence of your brand simply states grandeur and aspiration and, by association, esteem.

The simplicity of clarity is often held in the hands of ambiguity and paradox. Take the following two questions as an example: What is your magic number? When is enough, enough?

These two questions are often posed in negotiations. Their purpose is to ascertain where some sort of limit lies. What makes these questions gruelling is that you may not have considered your answer, thereby implicating you and the understanding of your worth. The design of these two questions and others similar to them invites ambiguity and paradox for the purpose of achieving advantage.

---

* *You can do a personal values assessment with the Barret Values Centre, which can be helpful if you are stuck* [22].

What do you mean?

Ambiguity is inexactness.

It occurs when there is more than one interpretation or possible solution for a word/concept/construct or situation. It happens where judgement and absolutes do not serve you as they move you towards cognitive distortion - another example of a situation where too much adrenaline will leave you wanting.

Being able to deal with obscurity and uncertainty with the absence of doubt requires mastery of skill obtained through training and the right chemistry.

In personal branding, depending on your positioning, there is space for clarity and vagueness in the same expression. There are times when you need to be able to pursue both options and times when you need to pursue neither and yet more times when you need to do one and not the other.

To have a successful luxurious experience with your personal brand, you need to make simplicity a paragon. Knowing what simplicity is and how to bring it about will provide your audience with the experience of luxury – a state of comfort and extravagance, singularity and choice. To create esteem and maintain simplicity, you should consider how you will support your audience when complexity (in the form of Ambiguity and Paradox) enters the room. With this in mind, knowing your magic number and when enough is enough creates chemistry.

Holding ambiguity in a paradoxical fashion may be the simplest way to hold the space – and this is a rare skill.

Ambiguity can be likened to building a puzzle, the picture may not be complete, yet you're able to work on the next piece of information based on what is available to you and to make decisions accordingly. When you're building a puzzle, the next piece that you pick up may not fit perfectly and would therefore be erroneous. Realising that you're off the mark and not forcing the piece into place is worth more than not acting at all. Finalising the puzzle is more about making decisions that lead to the completion of the picture than making no decisions or decisions that constantly bring the wrong piece to the table.

This is how business and branding are the same.

Permission to fail and succeed

I am curious – do you have permission to attempt and to make mistakes?

Permission introduces comfort with uncertainty. We spoke about safety earlier; comfort is another experience with the same theme.

Comfort and the lack of comprehensive information are ambiguous.

Having permission to make mistakes and being comfortable with inexactness offer you the opportunity to be comfortable with your discomfort as you invest in the confidence to deal with ambiguity. Increased levels of confidence and awareness in the face of ambiguous futures cultivate strength and character.

How flexible are you? Really? A principle of neurolinguistic programming (NLP) states, "The component/person with the most flexibility in a system controls the system" [23].

Ambiguity has a way of revealing facts randomly. Being able to adjust appropriately in the context of these 'new' findings is a gift in decision-making and directional changes.

> *"How will your personal brand 'do restraint' and allow for matters to unfold as they must?"*
>
> **– M. J. Nel –**

I mentioned intuition earlier when I spoke about the integration of your senses in your Personal Brand Sensory Framework. 'Listening to your gut' refers to how well you can pull information from the resources that your sensory systems provide as you need to make decisions in ambiguity.

The pressure of having to have the answers can be overwhelming. Having a council of advisors is another resource that allows you to present your case and listen to the wisdom and insight, with the alternative viewpoints enabling your brain and mind to craft another way forward.

I have made you aware of homoeostasis throughout S.U.I.T.S.™ and of how your mind, brain and body pursues it. Stressors in these three areas of your existence are therefore nothing new. Being at ease within the environment of ambiguity offers you a pathway to successfully dealing with problems and challenges.

Same side of the coin?

Paradox is self-contradiction where proof of the validity of the parts present is valid. In life and business, Paradox is ambiguity's cousin. It is where a statement/person/thing/situation inexplicably conflicts with and presents variance in its parts, yet is authentic in itself.

For example; you are both alive and dead. You have cells in your body that are regenerating and cells that are dead and on their way out. Your very existence is paradoxical. So, as a coach, when I'm asked to help people deal with paradox, I often revert to the client in the chair and ask how he/she does paradox.

After all, the client has been doing it for his/her whole life. The 'aha' moment that follows is priceless. The client now owns his/her thinking and ability to do paradox through the enabling conversation, the new resourced ability is embedded for life.

> *"The test of a first-rate intelligence is the ability to hold two opposite ideas in mind at the same time and still retain the ability to function..."*
>
> **– F. Scott Fitzgerald –**

As in the above example of life and death, you understand that we all have contradictory characteristics. The key is to find ways in which our core characteristics complement one another and to use them to improve our performance in challenging situations.

In her research, Kelle Olwyler, the co-author of "Paradoxical Thinking" shows that paradoxical components are two sides of the same coin (like a pendulum swinging from side to side). She goes on to say, "Accepting and valuing our paradoxes, as well as understanding those of people with whom we associate... is the process of consciously bringing together our two paradoxical sides to achieve outstanding results." [24]

In the preface of S.U.I.T.S.™, page 28, you created a set of new states from which you could practice your ability to hold paradox. You have essentially already synthesised these cognitive processes.

One of the things that gets in the way of holding paradox is cognitive distortion. An example is polarised thinking: either... or..., failure or success, life or death. This distortion causes the collapse of the middle ground, the dissipation of shades of grey. The distorted thinking leads to seeing yourself as a failure instead of celebrating your progress when you have fallen short in your performance.

When you hold paradox in personal branding, you offer your audience flexibility and, therefore, the ability to solve incongruence and keep face. You can also match your skill set and capabilities to the needs of your audience in an imaginative way - setting you apart from others and clearly differentiating you.

> *"All behavior consists of opposites. Learn to see things backward, inside out, and upside down."*
>
> **– Lao Tzu –**

Intelligence has seven components: logic and intuition, reason and imagination, memory, judgement and paradox. You may have noticed that the first four skills are paradoxical. This makes you an intelligent, dynamic inventor of constructs and solutions in your very being.

While you will be faced with ambiguity and paradox, your audience will face the same in relation to you and your brand. In the next section, when you're creating your Personal Brand Promise, consider how it can bring clarity and provide direction while offering others ample space to express and find their belonging. With paradox and ambiguity and your capabilities of them as a key resource, consider the promise that you want to make to yourself and others and complete the four levels of the brand promise, benefits, and features, matching them to your audience's needs.

TAILOR YOUR BRAND: PROMISE TO PROMISE

Use the following process to define and design your sacred promise in the form of your Personal Brand Glyph (a pictograph, character, or symbol).

To assist you, I have integrated two icons – the results looks similar to a mandala (a spiritual and ritual symbol). It lays yin-yang (a structure that integrates seemingly opposite or contrary forces, presenting them as complementary, interconnected, and interdependent – your world, your audience's world) over human needs in the context of branding, giving rise to a third universe as they interrelate.

The purpose of creating your sacred glyph is to offer you a way to develop a structure that enables a fluid mix of emotional, environmental and personal ingredients. As a result, you are relevant to your audience and can have meaningful conversations with long-term brand relationships.

The Sacred Glyph serves to create a totality of your promises, answering your audience's needs.

The levels that you consider for your sacred glyph should include the following: *

> • *Functional needs* – What pragmatic problem are you solving? What do you promise to do about it?
>
> • *Experiential needs* – What are your audience's practical and knowledge needs? What do you promise to share?
>
> • *Symbolic needs* – What virtue do they want represented in association with your brand? What do you promise to be?
>
> • *Metaphysical needs* – What abstract thought or subject (i.e. existence, truth, first principle, ultimate grounds) do you offer access to that appeals to their intellectual and philosophical needs? What are you ultimately promising?
>
> * *See 'f' under Notes and References.*

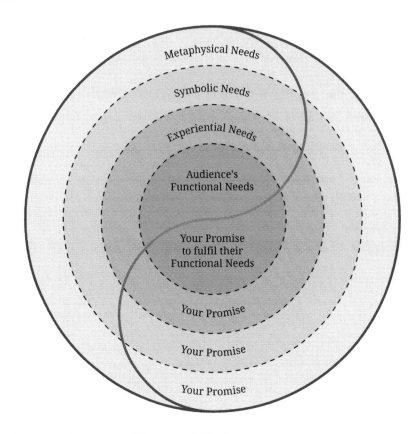

▲ *Diagram Five: Matt White Sacred Glyph™*

Having created your sacred glyph, you should review this article in the context of the other living documents. Check:

- That you're still on track with your personal brand manifesto;
- That you have not veered off your scope of work;
- That the impact on your personal brand charter is congruent in terms of your objectives, goals, and RASCI.

Financial Security: Products and services

With the creation of your sacred glyph, you have four areas for which you can create products and services. In certain instances, you may have a service or a product for every level; they may be related to each other but different. You may consider having one product or service to address all levels of your audience's needs.

TAILOR YOUR BRAND: YOUR UNIQUE BLEND

In your audience's mind, you're now offering distinctive elements that position you uniquely in an appealing manner; you are different from your competitors. As you populate the table below and create your blend of offerings, bear in mind the following regarding the product/service that addresses the client's needs:

- What makes you specifically credible?
- How is it relevant to the customer's need?
- Is the benefit clear and compelling?
- Does the value justify the price?

Sacred Glyph Level	Client Need	Product/ Service	As it relates to your credibility
Functional Needs			
Experiential Needs			
Symbolic Needs			
Metaphysical Needs			

▲ *Table Fourteen: Product/Service, Client Need Unique Blend*

TAILOR YOUR BRAND: THE VALUE OF UNIQUENESS

I bring the question, "How much is enough?", to you: not to negotiate, but so that you can consider your income requirement from your personal brand. This will assist in expectation management and afford you the comfort to commit to and live in a flourishing brand.

PART 1 With all the resources at your disposal, review your living artefacts as you consider the following:

- Have you allocated all your intrinsic and extrinsic resources' appropriately?
- How has the work that you have done so far impacted your schedule?
- To what extent are you tracking the work that lies ahead of you?
- Are you realistically identifying what is at risk?
- To what extent are you able to mitigate the risks that arise?

PART 2 Review your income and expense sheet and add your product and service lines; ensure that you calculate the following:

- Your ideal earnings from a new client at each level of your Sacred Glyph;
- The number of new clients you'll have in the next 24 months at each level of your Sacred Glyph;
- The average number of referrals you will receive from a new client over a period of 24 months;
- Do the calculation and add it to your income stream.

PART 3 The following parts will assist you in staying relevant as you innovate for and engage with your audience:

- *Research and development* – What have you realised is within your grasp to refine and create?
- *Processes* – Do you have the processes that enable your delivery and are required to support the products and services you created?
- *Channels* – Through which channels will your audience engage with you?
- With customer experience being central to processes, to what extent will your audience feel that the experience is designed for them? What enhancements do you need to bring about to achieve a customer-centric focus?

Consider the above and enhance your living artefacts accordingly.

The Three Musketeers

I am part of a circle of distinguished cavaliers. We esteem one another, respect each other's illustrious praises, and influence, celebrate, and support each other with our very essence. And you have now been invited into the inner circle. I would like to introduce you to Erik Kruger, the founder of Better Man and creator of PROJECT328 [25].

Erik's philosophy of creating a project framework that helps you achieve your goals within their contexts has its roots in Brian Moran and Michael Lennington's work, The 12 Week Year [26]. Brian and Michael advocate setting goals in a 12-week cycle to achieve the future and stay engaged. Being meticulous about supporting others to achieve their goals, Eric created the P328 framework which breaks the 90 days down even further.

He states, "Simply; you set 3 Moves (goals) that you want to work towards in the next 28 days". I personally believe that multitasking has not served anyone well and Eric, Brian, and Michael's approach to getting it done is the foundation for the next exercise and a way out of multitasking.

I promised at the outset that your Personal Brand would happen for you. Spreading yourself too thin dilutes your input and subsequently compromises your output and perceived value. This is not your aim. This approach supports you into action and creates momentum without diluting your progress and value.

✄ *TAILOR YOUR BRAND: READY, SET, GO!*

PART 1 In your S.U.I.T.S.™ Personal Brand Project Charter you have created several objectives/goals that you would like to achieve. Take the time now to put them into order so that they will create the steps and conclude the stages of establishing your brand.

PART 2 Once you have completed the steps and stages, order them in priority.

Take the prioritised list and convert each goal into actions which you will conclude in the next 28 days. The reason for the 28-day cycle is to support your sense of accomplishment, enable agile action, and enhance your adult-learning cycle.

Now consider which three goals will bring you closest to achieving your ideal state in the next 28 days. Place them in the S.U.I.T.S.™ Personal Brand Tactical Plan using the table below as a guideline.

Break the goals down into daily actions that will support the achievements of your goals. The 28-day cycle allows you to finish a piece of work, review actions required for the next 28-day cycle, and create, act on, and embed your personal brand behaviours.

Should you achieve your goals in a shorter time frame, you can reset the S.U.I.T.S.™ Personal Brand Tactical Plan and start a new 28-day cycle.

S.U.I.T.S.™ Personal Brand Tactical Plan

THEME: (from SOW)		GOAL 1: (from Charter)	OBJECTIVE: (from Charter)	GOAL 2: (from Charter)	Cycle Dates:	GOAL 3: (from Charter)	e.g. 1 Feb – 28 Feb
Activities/ Daily Actions	Time Milestones		Activities/ Daily Actions	Time Milestones		Activities/ Daily Actions	Time Milestones
Sensory Systems to activate/utilise	Values to activate/ draw on		Sensory Systems to activate/utilise	Values to activate/ draw on		Sensory Systems to activate/utilise	Values to activate/ draw on
Energy Zones to activate/utilise	Motivational ladder to activate/utilise		Energy Zones to activate/utilise	Motivational ladder to activate/utilise		Energy Zones to activate/utilise	Motivational ladder to activate/utilise
Tools that I can use	RASCI (who to involve)		Tools that I can use	RASCI (who to involve)		Tools that I can use	RASCI (who to involve)
Income I am expecting	Investment I need to incur		Income I am expecting	Investment I need to incur		Income I am expecting	Investment I need to incur

▲ Table Fifteen: S.U.I.T.S.™ Personal Brand Tactical Plan v1

The sophistication of relaxation

With ambiguity and paradox in the vault of understanding and your S.U.I.T.S.™ Personal Brand Tactical plan in full swing, I present you with the other side of work: play. As you may know, all work and no play…

Are you taking care of yourself with laughter and downtime? Take a minute to consider your four energy zones and calibrate the activities to include the appropriate enhancements and break-away planning. How would you reframe nutrition, hydration, fitness, and calibration so that the new frame would enable you to achieve your ultimate intent?

As you review the four energy zones, become aware of how your personal brand sensory integration framework influences and supports the sophistication of relaxation towards the healthy-and-well state of your mind-body loop.

In summary

The totality of your being is integrated through the senses, which provide you with data to recalibrate your personal brand and behavioural framework.

A massive transformational vision supported by an agile strategy and a coinciding tactical plan is foundational to achieving business and brand success.

To achieve iconic leadership in part is to embrace your humanity and shortcomings while you partner exceptional resources to achieve exponential impact.

Purpose with action creates the foundation for healthy chemistry and neuroplasticity.

Simplifying paradox and ambiguity creates comfort for your audience and underpins the luxury experience of your brand.

Being able to create multiple levels of expectation through the alignment of your brand promise to your audience's need offers you the opportunity to engage as you provide value.

A leader who has vision but lacks action is a definitive daydreamer.

Balancing work with play supports your wellness chemistry and allows for a higher level of achievement and motivation.

What is in the next chapter?

- You can look forward to your impact on people as an iconic leader.
- Create a networking plan that supports your income aspirations and your social impact.
- Investigate outlining your stakeholder interaction framework.
- Interrogating your audience and creating a target market strategy. ⊗

MATT WHITE

UNITERNITY

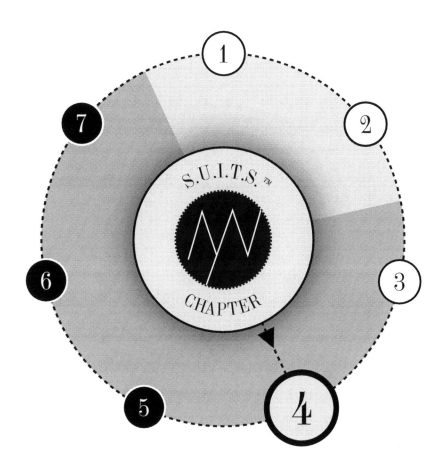

MATT WHITE

CHAPTER FOUR

Activate it – Uniternity: The universe and eternity

Your second portmanteau is Uniternity; it is the coalition between your universe and eternity.

It is defined as "a state of all that exists as a whole (activity, interest, experience) to which time has no application (timelessness) in the context of ever expansion."

The reason why someone would think that they were and mostly behave like they were the centre of the universe fascinates me because it is paradoxical. Often, the person doesn't understand the paradox of it.

> *"Today, right now, who you are and who you want to be, is becoming one".*
>
> **– M. J. Nel –**

Creating a personal brand, challenging as it is, is a small task compared to, say, creating a galaxy in a universe, let alone being the centre or creator of the universe.

But I suppose, as is the case with most matters, it is a point of view.

With the pressure to be the nucleus of the universe, I wonder if you could be so much more?

What if being that centre is a limiting move in the context of eternity?

That brings me to my next question; "What do you really want?"

Uniternity is about finding how you relate to the other forces present in your reality, specifically people, and how the promises that you made in Strasion create and support a universe of sorts. Learning how your cosmos worked was a voyage you undertook in chapter 1 – neuroplasticity. Learning what you wanted was part of the work you did in the preface and chapter 2. Learning how you were going to create it was the work that you did in chapter 3. So, in summary, the work you have completed was internally focused. With Uniternity, you begin the journey of boldly going where no one has gone before [27].

To be specific, in Uniternity, you'll focus on defining your target audience, refining your stakeholders, and reviewing your relationships. This is an integral part of personal branding as people are the universe within which you will be operating and your relationships with them will touch on the eternal – is this enough paradox to keep you engaged?

People in the Context of Iconic Leadership

Before I became involved in neuroscience and neuro-semantics, I did not understand what caused some people to be inherently motivated and others to need inspiration just to get out of bed. To me, that there were different types of people was a mere fact of existence as was how I got on with my day.

Whenever I encountered the second type of person, I used to think, "Get on with it, will you?" This statement should give you an idea of how deep my neuro-fear-based action-oriented-bias was.

Motivating and encouraging people is foundational to iconic leadership and a compelling vision goes a long way towards providing the necessary inspiration. Before I continue about people in the context of iconic leadership, I present you with what I term to be inspiration and motivation.

Motivation refers to your reasons (choices) for behaving in a particular way based on your expectations regarding the results of the behaviour [28]. Inspiration refers to the mental stimulation necessary to feel or do something.

That makes inspiration a fundamental pillar in this book. Hence, you have invested the time and energy in using S.U.I.T.S.™ as a methodology to determine what makes you inspiring.

To your inspiring self, we will add the motivation and enthusiasm necessary for your audience to make your brand a success.

The reason for creating four levels of meaning and audience interaction in your sacred glyph is to provide a source of sustained energy. From this, your audience can draw enthusiasm as it embarks on interacting with your products and services and the changes that your products and services will bring to its environment. Simultaneously, you gain the opportunity to interact with your audience around different decisions.

As an effective personal brand, you will raise different levels of expectations that a) engaging with your product/service will bring about superior results and b) results will lead to rewarding and irresistible outcomes. Therefore, you're creating the energy that rewards intrinsic (meaning) and extrinsic (performance) factors, making your brand relevant and tangible.

What was the state you created for this section of the book in the preface? Can you fully access it now? Is it still the most resourceful state for you to use? Is it everything that you have become aware of? How do you rate your iconic leadership ability?

Networthing: Exchanging self-worth and adding value

The first time I come across Networthing, it was part of a screensaver at a Lifestyle club. The word delighted me. So, I waited in eager anticipation to see what the meaning of the neologism would be on the slideshow. I waited in vain until the slides started looping. Then I made a mental note to search for its meaning. What I found made me contemptuous. Its definition boiled down to profiting from relationships – almost a method of making money using people that involved delayed gratification – like the cunning act of an emissary. So, I humbly propose to redefine this portmanteau, which I did not create, as I believe it has value for the purpose of personal branding.

Hence, I propose that networthing means adding worth (knowledge, talent, resources, etc.) to relationships (interacting with people in a personal and professional capacity) towards a purpose (others, community etc.) so as to affect an increase in value without expecting recompense. The new definition precludes the possible result of the original intent of networthing (monetary gain) but implies being in service. So, after redefining the word, I have found that it was the intention implied in the original definitions that was disagreeable, not the result.

In the Triangles Model™ [12], Dr. Weinberg proves the point that integration between professional and business relationships is fundamental for the good chemistry and subsequent neuroplasticity of the individual.

In my META work (the structure of meaning), I have seen the mitigation of several destructive cognitive patterns through integrated relationships. Integrated relationships bring into the equation the value of a different point of view from a safe trusted source.

As you invest time in people, sharing experiences professionally and personally, offering a sincere and honest connection increases the memorability of the conversation. Sustaining that connection through a resourceful level of trust, implied and applied, bridges the gap and builds brand equity, thereby transcending time. When your intent for the interaction is clear, the true value of networthing comes to life.

The S.U.I.T.S.™ personal branding model provides a platform that seamlessly transitions touchpoints (conversations, products/services/interactions) between transactional (tactics) through transformational action (influencing) into transworth (value/leadership) experience. Networthing is therefore an inclusive component of personal branding. There is more about this in ***TAILOR YOUR BRAND: ESSENTIAL RELATIONSHIPS.***

At the heart of profit and loss

Paradoxically, I believe that relationships are an asset. Simply put, they have value. In my world, assets help me meet my commitments, grow my legacy, and increase my ability to make a difference. As any good accountant will tell you, assets can depreciate or appreciate in value. Have you considered the status of your inner circle asset registry and its corresponding value?

What do you know about how you construct relationships? What blinkers obscure your vision of how you set up, maintain, and close out relationships. Do you understand the difference between toxic and supplemental relationships? How do you nurture each type of relationship? What do you want more of and what do you want less of?

These questions are designed to help you think through your relationship asset registry. To accelerate the process, I have created a three-part exercise to address your inner circle.

With a clearly crafted sacred glyph declaring your promise to the world, understanding how you construct relationships is the next step in your protocol.

✂ *TAILOR YOUR BRAND: ESSENTIAL RELATIONSHIPS*

PART 1   Use the table provided:

Decide on a list of constructs, i.e., trust, transparency, mutual intent, safety, ethics, reward, etc., that are non-negotiable in relationships. You can have as many or as few constructs as you require.

Explore how constructs are applicable to both professional and personal relationships.

Place the constructs in the relevant columns in the table. Should you decide that your construct is relevant in both the professional and personal environments, you can merge the two columns into one.

Write the names of the people whom you are in relationship with in the Name column.

Now rate your experience of the relationship using the guidelines of the constructs out of a 100.

Use the total column to aggregate an average score.

S.U.I.T.S.™ Relationship Matrix								
	Personal				**Professional**			
Name	e.g. Trust	e.g. Safety	e.g. Mutual Intent	TOTAL	e.g. Ethics	e.g. Reward	e.g. Honesty	TOTAL

▲ *Table Sixteen: S.U.I.T.S.™ Relationship Matrix*

PART 2   Using the S.U.I.T.S.™ Relationship Matrix, diagram six, page 110, populate your relationship inventory. Allow the following thought processes to guide your thinking: The middle point of the circle represents you: the centre of your relationship universe with a score of 100.

The x-axis divides the diagram below into half, and the y-axis divides it into quarters.

Decide which of the halves represent your professional relationships and which ones represent your personal relationships on the x-axis or use the diagram as created.

Decide on which half represents resourceful relationships and which half represents relationships that need review on the y-axis.

Lastly, decide on the minimum score that would be the outside circle score. Now you can decide what to do with the relationship that scored less than your minimum score and act accordingly

PART 3   I am intrigued to know what you have realised now that you have a visual representation of how you allocate your time (investment) and its results.

Consider your living artefacts as well as your energy zones and sensory brand framework, and apply the impact of your realisations to reflect the necessary changes.

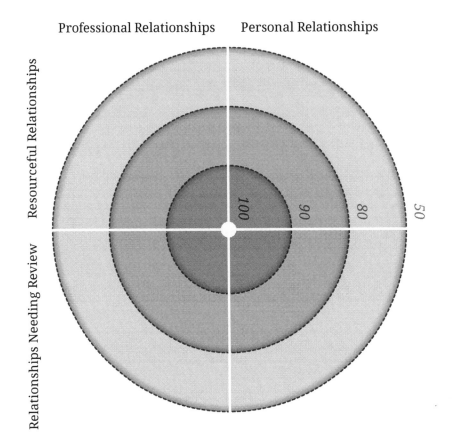

Professional Relationships   Personal Relationships

Resourceful Relationships

Relationships Needing Review

100 90 80 50

▲ *Diagram Six: S.U.I.T.S.™ Relationship Matrix*

Creating abundance

Before I continue to discuss stakeholder management, I would like to talk about the surplus economy.

In personal branding, a surplus is defined as the presence of super-abundance – abundance above and beyond the required tax of action (cost of being/doing something). There is a wealth of well-documented information regarding the surplus economy phenomenon. The piece that I would like to bring to your attention relates to the surplus of people for the available jobs in the market. Your S.U.I.T.S.™ personal branding journey is about making you essential to the future economic platform and creating your independence from it – paradox and ambiguity in action. One of the pillars of creating abundance for yourself has to do with how you conduct the relationships you choose.

How does your state of lack or the abundance of the type of quality relationship that you require contribute to your ultimate intent? When you are in a state of surplus relationships, what is the state of your professional and personal health? How does this abundance of relationships experience your promises and value addition?

Lack in and of itself is not a negative. It offers a platform for your reevaluation of the state in which there is lack. If this state is perpetual, you may find yourself in a spot of bother. My question to you follows: In what way does lack offer you an opportunity to achieve your highest intent to live your ultimate life and be the legend that you are?

One of the factors that contributes to the successful creation of abundance could be stakeholder management. For S.U.I.T.S.™ personal branding work, a stakeholder is a person who has a vested interest in your success. People, not organisations, are stakeholders. The people in question may lead organisations or head departments, but the organisations are not stakeholders.

As management in the organisational context means illustrating a process of control, it can include supporting a state of fear, I propose that you consider Stakeholder Organics. Organic stakeholder engagement refers to the practices that strive to cycle resources (time, money, people, etc.), pursue ecological balance (that which is most resourceful for the state of abundance of the system), and conserve diversity (in people, thought, culture, etc.).

Stakeholder Organics: A Farmer's Approach

I grew up on a farm near Polokwane in the Limpopo Province of South Africa in the previous millennium. The family farm was home to livestock (cattle, sheep, horses, rabbits, chicken) and an array of wild animals (foxes, bucks, hogs, tortoises, and snakes). Our existence was simplistic but did not resemble anything simple. The dynamics of growing crops (maize, vegetables, lucerne) were challenging given the drought (of the early 1980s) and the financial institutions' uncompromising stance. It was here, in the merciless grip of drought, in the hands of the guardians of life (the labourers and chiefs of the local tribes) and with the fierceness of laws (families, institutions, politics) that I was instructed in the fine art of organic influence and repurposing lack.

The long-term success of the farm was built on friendship. The insight that these relationships brought was priceless. The benefits that statecraft wielded (the relationship between the financial institution and the farm) were marginal in comparison and often led to lost battles. What is the essence of the most influential relationships in your matrix? More importantly, what are you going to do about nurturing it?

To support your crafting of a crystal clear RASCI model that you can incorporate into your project charter and apply to your tactical plan, create a table and consider the following:

- Name your stakeholders.
- What are their keen interests?
- What issues are they tackling or defending?
- What level of support do you require from them?
- With what actions are you positioning yourself as a solution to the issues they want to advance on?
- What message do they need to hear from you?
- How you will get to them, communicate with them?

It is all about timing

A key consideration about stakeholders is the time needed to achieve the results that you want, how that fits into their diaries, and the level of urgency of the benefits that your products/services will bring them. Devising a practical plan that communicates the appropriate information in a way that others do not and delivering it in a way that uniquely positions it as credible at the right time is invaluable.

Would a story without an antagonist be worth telling? Isn't the hero's journey to the summit and overcoming of the hitherto insurmountable challenge at the heart of what is encouraging? Neutralising the opposition and providing proof to the sceptics is what you will do through your stakeholder organics.

With the results from the matrix about the relationships that you foster, you gained insight as you identified key stakeholders in your personal brand. In addition, you gained insight into your communication style and the information that stakeholders would need to support you to achieve your ultimate intent. The next section focuses on customer relationships, your ideal target market.

Splitting apples – a target market practice

Being able to aim your arrows at the target of success, is as much about nailing your intention as it is about receiving a reward.

The iterations of the story of William Tell vary from one culture to another. The expert marksman was able to shoot an apple that was balanced on the head of one of his own over what seemed to be an impossible distance for the reward of freedom under the instruction and scrutiny of the King.

That was quite a feat. The metaphor is true for the achievement of slicing your target market. The components include:

- Being unwavering in your abilities (marksmanship),
- Being passionately clear about your target (the apple),
- Fully understanding the consequences of your actions (the impact on the life of one of your own should you miss),
- Enjoying the reward (freedom),
- Knowing what is expected of you (splitting the apple),
- The audience you maintain (the king and the village people).

> *"You are the authority on You.*
> *Which means you are the one best equipped in choosing your trade*
> *(products and services) and your tools.*
> *But your audience will be the ones to decide which unlocks their homage".*
>
> *– M. J. Nel –*

Once you fulfil all these elements of your story, you will have crafted the stuff that legends are made of.

Having a clear definition of your target market allows you to focus your marksmanship (effort and resources) with a specific brand message (freedom in this case) as it illustrates the benefits of engaging you.

How you do it is the fabric of the stories that people tell and why your brand will become part of their existence.

Before I take you into target market creation, let's look at what your products and services are.

TAILOR YOUR BRAND: A CURIOUS CASE OF APPLES AND PEARS

Use the following table to accelerate your understanding of your products and services where:

- Features are understood as the distinctive attributes that make the product/service unique;
- Benefits are understood as the advantage that the use of the product/service brings;

- META benefits are understood as the meaning the benefits you bring to your audience;
- Value is understood as the problem/challenge that the use of the product/ service solves, alleviates.

	S.U.I.T.S.™ Delivery Mechanism							
Description	*Products*				*Service*			
	Features	Benefits	META Benefit	Value	Features	Benefits	META Benefit	Value

▲ *Table Seventeen: Products and Services*

The table above provides you with an inventory – apples and pears. With your basket of fresh produce, ask the question, "Who is ready for the results that the META benefits would bring?", and infuse your living artefacts and adjust your relationship asset register.

Who goes to the market?

Answering the question about who is ready for your offering is the starting point for the exploration of your primary target market. Now create a target market matrix to define your ideal client and where you can find him or her by first considering the following in the context of your offering:

- In your current audience, who will yield in the achievement of your personal brand goals?
- What trends can you identify in the characteristics and interests of this audience?
- When you evaluate your competitors, who is their current customer base? How will the inclusion of their customers enrich your audience – if at all?
- As you consider your competitors and their customer base, is there a glaring gap in the market that you could focus your efforts on?

You now have a rough draft of your Target Market. Now refine it.

✂ *TAILOR YOUR BRAND: TARGET PRACTICE*

PART 1 Thinking through the following – what are the audience members' ages, genders, locations, educational levels, income positions, family statuses, professional occupations, ethnic backgrounds, and any additional demographics which you feel are relevant to completing your exercise.

PART 2 Enhancing the table with the following psychographics: interests and hobbies, lifestyle requirements, professional behaviours and habits, what they value, and their attitudes.

PART 3 Deciding who constitute your primary target audience and your secondary market.

PART 4 Writing a paragraph that summarises each of your primary and secondary target markets, explaining which product/service fits within their lifestyles. Is there a gap in their lives/lifestyles that you could fill? As you craft this narrative, consider which features of your offering are most appealing to them.

Are you clear on which media they turn to for information and how they think about their need?

To test the viability of your product in the context of your target market paragraphs, apply the 'toothbrush test' as Larry Page, the co-founder of Google developed it. How will your product/service be used twice a day to enhance the ultimate experience of whatever it is that your target market is trying to achieve?

PART 5 With your target markets identified, make the qualification that they are viable in size and can afford your product/service.

Being able to relate to your target market and define it as best you can is taxing. A clear definition of whom you want to do business with will enable you to enjoy the rewarding effort of designing the media and the message for connecting with them in Timmulation (Chapter 6).

Mountains and Molehills?

> *"There is no way to happiness – happiness is the way".*
>
> **– Thich Nhat Hanh –**

Joseph Campbell was the American scholar who authored "Hero's Journey" [29]. In his work, he described the phases that the hero of a story would typically journey through. According to Campbell, once the hero embraced his discomfort and accepted his call to action, he could set out against mighty odds.

The ordeal that he faced had many names, and in most if not all cases, sacrifice was required.

I place before you that pivotal point:

> • What must you be prepared to give up to achieve your highest intent?
> • What difficulty must you overcome but haven't had the courage to?
> • How is this related to what is holding you back?
> • What have you been unwilling to embrace that might contain your vitality elixir?

As your Personal Brand Master, I am asking if you're turning molehills into mountains and missing the journey of happiness? Because the time is right for your mission – review and amplify your living artefacts in the context of the questions above.

✂ *TAILOR YOUR BRAND: IN THE MIX*

Consider your S.U.I.T.S.™ Personal Brand Tactical Plan and enhance it with your target market and products and services in the following table:

S.U.I.T.S.™ Personal Brand Tactical Plan

THEME: (from SOW)		OBJECTIVE: (from Charter)	Cycle Dates:

GOAL 1: (from Charter)		GOAL 2: (from Charter)		GOAL 3: (from Charter)	
Activities/ Daily Actions	Time Milestones	Activities/ Daily Actions	Time Milestones	Activities/ Daily Actions	Time Milestones
Sensory Systems to activate/utilise	Values to activate/ draw on	Sensory Systems to activate/utilise	Values to activate/ draw on	Sensory Systems to activate/utilise	Values to activate/ draw on
Energy Zones to activate/utilise	Motivational ladder to activate/utilise	Energy Zones to activate/utilise	Motivational ladder to activate/utilise	Energy Zones to activate/utilise	Motivational ladder to activate/utilise
Tools that I can use	RASCI (who to involve)	Tools that I can use	RASCI (who to involve)	Tools that I can use	RASCI (who to involve)
Target Market	Product Service match	Target Market	Product Service match	Target Market	Product Service match
Income I am expecting	Investment I need to incur	Income I am expecting	Investment I need to incur	Income I am expecting	Investment I need to incur

▲ Table Eighteen: S.U.I.T.S.™ Personal Brand Tactical Plan v2

In summary - Chapter Four

Your personal brand exists in eternity and you are the master of the universe you create.

As an Iconic Leader your ability to motivate, inspire and encourage yourself and others is key to success.

Your personal brand commodities and assets span across your products, services, and relationships.

Being able to provide different types of interactions for your audience through a variety of touch points makes your brand interesting.

Stakeholder engagement through the change process is about meaning and value. Clearly answer the question "What is in it for me?" for your audience.

What is in the next chapter?

- Together we will burnish your Identity's facets.
- You will create a power zone matrix.
- As part of Strasion and Uniternity, you will implement a brand matrix.
- Explore the variety of Brand Archetypes at your disposal.
- Define your healing qualities. ⓦ

MATT WHITE

I DENION

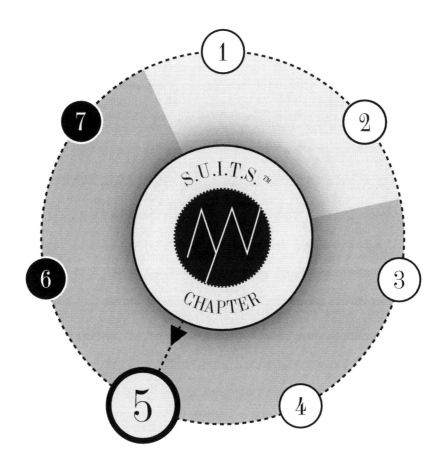

MATT WHITE

CHAPTER FIVE

Craft it - Idenion; your Identity for Dominion

Your third portmanteau is the fusion of your identity and dominion; Idenion.

Idenion is "the fact of your sovereignty in destiny".

As a member of a small cohort, Generation X (Harvard Center, 1965-1984), shifting societal values is nothing new.

> *"Always in motion is the future".*
>
> **– YODA, Star Wars Episode V: The Empire Strikes Back –**

Not knowing what the future has to offer is familiar. Financial struggle, parental absense or loss are examples as a latchkey kid traumas. Personally, I decided to not let my own traumas deter me from taking ownership, creating a happy and active life, and achieving work-life harmony amidst the lack of adult guidance.

Like a Cohors sagittaria (a Roman infantry auxiliary unit of bowmen), I have no qualms about shooting fiery darts. Being an alienated youth (part of the lost generation) and not having a name for 30 years (as the statistician didn't know what to call us) increased my desire for identity (to know who I was) and dominion (to know what was mine). What the generations before us and after us lacked in entrepreneurial abilities, we made up for. Not knowing where we belonged taught us a valuable skill, being many things to many people. That very skill is our Achilles heel: the craving for identity caused us to remain lost when we did not take up our hero's journey to find our true identity.

In my work, I found that Gen X was not the only part of the population that was seeking the truth.

Power in the Context of the Iconic Leader

My fellow cohort members and I need others who are in relationship with us not to confuse authority with leadership. Authority exists by default/design, leadership is what I give you through my submission.

Leaders who rely on their ability to discipline and reward as a means of influence/authority miss out on the power of gaining integrity and admiration by being experts in their fields (as a way of leading).

Obtaining the best from those who entrust you with direction depends on your source of power and your understanding of it.

The research of social psychologists, John French and Bertram Raven [30], provided a timeless script for leaders to understand the influence of power, prepare for it, govern with it and honour the basis from which people submitted to it. The original study defined five forms of the basis of power and was later enriched with a sixth form.

According to the study, 1) legitimate power outlines the belief that a person has a formal right to make demands whilst expecting others to comply with obedience; 2) the power of reward results in one's ability to compensate another for compliance; 3) obtaining expert power is based on a high level of skill and knowledge, while 4) reverent power is the result of the perception of another's worthiness of respect. The belief that one can be punished for non-compliance results in 5) coercive power and, finally, 6) information power, the control of information which others need to achieve accomplishment.

French and Raven split the basis of power into two zones, positional power and personal power.

The positional power zones included legitimate, reward, coercive, and information power, while personal power comprised expert and reverent power.

> *"I wonder if the Personal branding phenomena arose from the ashes of people being lost in themselves and wanting belonging?"*
>
> – M. J. Nel –

Examples of holders of legitimate power include a president, a CEO, and a general. This form of power mandates election (political, military, economic, etc.) or appointment (social, cultural, religious). Its weakness lies in its unpredictability and instability as influence is based on position rather than on whom you are. This sphere of power is limited to situations where others believe one has the right to influence and control. To give an example, a traffic officer instructing one person to be more courteous towards another is likely to be ignored, while a priest could have better success with the same directive, illustrating the importance of context for this form of power.

Legitimate power is often part of a two-edged sword; reward power constitutes the other side of the sword. People in high positions are often able to give rewards. These can range from compliments to assignments, opportunities, and promotions, as well as financial recompense. If the expectation is that you will be rewarded for doing what a leader wants, there is a high probability that you will comply. The duality that defines this power base often hides the severity of the implications, for instance, complete control of promotion, increases etc.

This power base's limitation finds itself in the perception of value in the mind's eye of the affected audience. The source of power can prove to be a valuable tool, but if it is weak, the perception of the audience can shift.

Coercive power is corrosive. Water and oxygen may be vital for the body, but corrosive for steel. A sure blade, leadership (and power) will implore justice to hear the lamentations of the people that it rules in order for all concerned to flourish. Amongst the expressions of coercive power are threats, punishment, intimidation, manipulation and control. What corrodes this powerbase further is not the need for legitimate discipline but the fact that the legitimate foundation can be poisoned by the many well-intentioned expressions of justice that shape infliction.

Information is particularly powerful in the connection economy. Being the custodian of information places you in quite a unique situation. The power base is not derived from the data itself but from the control of the aqueduct. Withholding and poisoning (manipulating, distorting, concealing) the water supply brought fortified cities to their knees and was a powerful weapon in warfare. Doing the same with the flow of data when it is a basic need for others to survive and flourish will surely see their Rome burn.

In the current economy, power is easy to obtain and hard to maintain.

As an Iconic Leader, supplementing the more resourceful positional power zones with complementary personal power sources indicates the depth of your groundwater, which will safeguard you in a season of siege.

Outperforming other leaders involves a grid of skill and knowledge. It draws on your ability to assess situations, offer solutions, provide conclusive discernment, truly listen, and earn trust. Leaders who are their subject matter experts command confidence, inspire ideas, bring value, and have reputations for 'thinking'. The expert power base is a revitalising spring that continually renews others. It pools longevity and regard for an iconic leader too.

Fondness and esteem for others because you identify with them in some ways make you susceptible to referent power. This power base is bestowed on you – it is a reward, not an achievement but an honour. Often the honour is bestowed based on an emotional connection as opposed to foundational merit. Holding referent power forges a powerful lightsabre of influence, commanding sobriety and responsibility. When the crack in your armour is a lack of integrity, honesty, and consistency you may alienate people and dilute their reverence for you.

Starting with the work on Idenion – reflect on the state that you created in the preface of S.U.I.T.S.™. What was that state? Can you fully access it now? Is it still the most resourceful state for you to use? Is it everything that you have become aware of? How do you rate your iconic leadership ability?

🎗 *TAILOR YOUR BRAND: POWER MATRIX*

Consider French and Raven's power bases and create a scorecard that best matches your current context and provides guidelines for how it will change as you migrate into your future. Use the following as you create the scorecard:

1. Use your personal brand manifesto as the guiding purpose statement. To activate the appropriate power matrix to move ahead with your aspirations, ensure that you look at what you're going to do (your objective), how you're going to be successful (your advantage), and where you're going to do it (your scope).

2. Aligning with your change agenda, what do you need to shift to make the world a better place for you first? How will you graphically represent it? What power basis will come to play inadvertently?

3. Review your translation point and paint a clear picture of the power strategy that you need to engineer.

4. With the Sacred Glyph, you can anticipate the needs of your audience. Which power base are they naturally inclined to that authentically aligns with your personal brand? How will you measure the effectiveness of your power matrix in your personal brand manifestation?

5. Use the agile approach and try the power matrix you created.

Idenion is about your signature

Idenion is your culture, it is your distinctive authority. It is how you do what you do because of who you are. It honours the fact that you are much more than a personal brand or the iconic leader whom you aspire to be. It is about embracing the person you have chosen to be and become, resisting the lie of personality, and embracing its fluidity.

I have awe for my father's signature: the authority that it carries, the actions it enforces, and the commands it gives. I remember attempting to forge it as a schoolboy when I needed it to confirm that I'd done my homework or on arbitrary communications from school that I'd either omitted to share with him or honestly forgotten to share. Distinctly, in these memories, I experienced the vile taste of impersonation. I just could not reconcile myself to pretending to be someone else, and that awareness was OK.

I vowed to become the person I needed to be for my own sake and that my future signature would carry the same simplistic power I adored in my father's signature. I would live with the consequences of being me.

Children search for inspiration for their signatures and attempt many iterations of them. As a grown man, I understand the gravitas of consistency and black ink. Your personal brand signature will mutate over the years of its existence. Idenion is about enabling further mutation into reliability. Your signature is a guarantee and a promise, that you will act with integrity and honour towards your commitments.

The fluidity of personality

Personality tests and psychometrics constitute a way in which businesses standardise how people behave as a result of what they think. I firmly believe that the person you are (your state of persona) is a set of choices that you have embedded into your behaviour, and now you refer to yourself by saying, "It is just the way I am – it is my personality". Yeah, right. What if I told you, you created you the way you wanted to be? In doing so, you have adopted a sort of passive aggressive stance as you serve your underlying narcissistic traits.

When you ask Michael Hall, Ph.D. (Cognitive Psychology), about personality, he answers with the following words:

> "Personality is what we do, not what we are. You and I do personality – it is how we think, emote, speak (language), act, and relate. As we do these things – we establish in our minds and the minds of others what we call our 'personality.' It's how people know us, recognize us, and think about us." [31]

So personality is about how you know yourself and how others think about you. What would the possibilities be if you explored the parts of you that you didn't know and the ways in which you hadn't functioned and incorporated the best of what you found and had to offer towards your highest intent?

The source of your learning to think, feel, speak, and act stems from all the influences you've experienced throughout your life. What makes up your 'personality' is the set of attributes which you have chosen, which have given you the current results.

When would be the best time to consider the alternative? How long do you want to carry on the way you have – being limited? When will the results you truly want, replace the ones that you currently have, thanks to your changing how you do you?

Taking his lead from Abraham Maslow in his book, *Toward a Psychology of Being* (1968), Dr. Hall indicates the following:

"Personality is context relative. You do your personality in some context in order to adjust or not to adjust and a healthy, strong, and vigorous sense of self can be deemed good in one context and a disorder in another.

So, if you learn to do personality, and if personality arises in specific contexts and is relative to those contexts – this implies several really important things. It is important to create healthy contexts. Parents, take note. School administrators, leaders, managers, etc., take note too. The context which you create for people to live and operate in inevitably has tremendous effects on the personalities they develop. Is it a healthy self-actualising context? Is it an unhealthy context? Is it loving or joyful? Does it promote learning, does it contribute to their lives, etc.?

Personality can positively change for the better. It is an ongoing process, so improving one's thinking, emoting, speaking, acting, and relating improves, enhances, and enriches one's personality. People are not stuck or victims of their fate.

How you know and express yourself is under your control – if you so choose. 'Personality' is not a mysterious force which is imposed on you. You may have tendencies and you may be wired to display certain talents, but you are not fated to 'be' a certain way. You can choose what to think and value and believe." [31]

Side-bar

Despite the perceived evil that stereotypes are responsible for, allow me to show you how you can use them to your advantage. By definition, stereotypes are oversimplified images or ideas of particular nouns. They are clichés that can serve you in that they provide you with a formula for communication. A personality can be one: I will explore the benefit of communicating through archetypes, which constitute a type of resourceful stereotype.

A diamond in the rough

A rough diamond is nothing to behold. All things considered, it could be a milky, murky glass shard.

Robin and Styne coined the lyrics to "Diamonds are a girl's best friend," [32] and Norma Jean's performance made it legendary. Queen Mary, Queen Elizabeth II, and my grandmother apparently shared the sentiment. During my early teens, my grandparents moved to a small town called Cullinan, 19 miles east of Pretoria, in the Highveld of Gauteng. The South African Province of Gauteng is known for its afternoon thunderstorms in the summer and splendid weather all year round.

The town's claim to fame was that the Cullinan Diamond, the largest rough diamond ever found, was discovered at a local mine on 26 January, 1905, and given to King Edward VII as his 66th birthday gift.

The stone was subsequently cut into several polished gems, the largest of which was named the Great Star of Africa. It was mounted in the head of the English Sovereign's Sceptre with Cross, indicating the Sovereign's temporal power as head of state. I guess we will never know whether steadfast love is guaranteed with the gift of a diamond but it is undeniable that this gemstone is mythical in its majesty.

N.W. Ayer & Son, an advertising agency, was founded in Pennsylvania in 1869. It is said that the firm convinced Americans that a diamond was the ultimate symbol of eternal love, romance, and commitment. Diamonds weren't always rare stones because, inherently, burnt wood was not worth much. Hence, the British financiers of the South African diamond mines needed to link diamonds to something a whole lot more valuable. The stereotype that existed in the late 1930s was that diamonds were reserved for the inordinately wealthy as an expression of their luxury. What essentially happened was that, in the declining market, a piece of carbon gained a psychological attribute that spoke to a fundamental human need. That fundamental need transcended its core to supersede Maslow's entire motivational ladder.

The post-war period, with the memory of loss fresh in everyone's mind, offered a rare opportunity to connect the most valuable experience for every human being (to love and to be loved in return) to a polished stone, thereby amplifying the stone's meaning and subsequent value. From mediaeval times, engagement rings were fairly common. However, immediately after the Allied victory, only 10% of engagement rings featured diamonds. So what was the plan? To convince a young man that the way to express his worth, was with a diamond ring, pledging his undying commitment and true love forever?

How can a stereotype serve you? In the same way that "A Diamond is Forever" served De Beers. Personal branding is not dissimilar to diamond cutting and polishing. Appropriate the piece of carbon that will illuminate your vision (yourself in this case), decide on the number of stones that you would like to cut from it (products and services), design its facets (features), polish it, and voila: 'true' love (the benefits of doing business with you).

The Personal Brand Experience Scorecard was designed to help you further the delight that you could evoke with your audience and the fulfilment that you would experience in life.

To get you started, I shall introduce you to a few stereotypes for your arsenal.

Carl Jung understood that a stereotype, a.k.a. an archetype, was an archaic pattern derived from a collection of unconscious competencies. When you become aware of the manifest behaviours, interactions, and impact of archetypes, you can draw from the content, conjuring images and actions with your audience that authentically represent you with little effort – this maximises stereotypes.

I am a firm believer in minimum input for maximum output. In this way, I align with Jung.

The original idea for the theory comes from work by Immanuel Kant, Plato and Arthur Schopenhauer. The thing which makes archetypes powerful (for good and evil) is that they are common to all cultures and your audience will relate to them as its members experience their own lives, texturing their thoughts, feelings, beliefs, and identities.

Below are some examples that I used in this chapter. In each case, the Jungian archetype follows the stereotype I used: Yoda – the Sage; Roman Cohort – Warrior; Iconic Leader – Leader; Father – Patriarch; Schoolboy – Child; Doctor – Healer/Magician; King Edward VII – King.

Consider what images came to mind as you read the words. This is what you will do when you access authentic archetypes that match your personal brand promise. In short, you have experienced the credibility that an archetype can lend you and that which you obtain with context.

When you're buying a diamond, the four C's are your guideline: carat, colour, cut, and clarity. Similarly, in the S.U.I.T.S.™ personal branding framework, the four C's represent the following: carat – purpose, colour – archetype, cut – products and services, and clarity – culture. The next two sections will deal with the archetype and culture of your 'forever' promise.

❀ *TAILOR YOUR BRAND: PERSONAL BRAND ARCHETYPE EXPERIENCE*

The following table provides you with key character traits of what I would term "Aspirational Archetypes" from Jungian theory.

PART 1 Use the table to create your own unique Archetype blend for your personal brand.

Read through the list and select three archetypes that point to your essence and non-negotiable character traits. Now mark them in order of hierarchy.

Describe how others would gain proof that you were expressing this archetype and connect with it in your context: what they would see, what they would hear you say (the words you would use), and how they would feel in relation to your products and services, which met their needs.

S.U.I.T.S.™ Personal Brand Experience

Archetype Names	The archetype's narrative	The archetype's key words	Proof		Connection	
			Visual (images that you would use to reflect your brand would show...)	Data (examples of words that you would use to evoke this archetype in your personal brand communication...)	Emotive (what your audience would feel)	Valuative (how this meets your audience's needs)
Genius/ Catalyst/ Healer	Empowerment, transformation, turning dreams into reality, knowledge of how the world works, developing vision and living it.	Miracle worker Intelligent Analytical Insightful				
Warrior/ Hero/ Crusader/ Olympian	Courage, self-belief, exerting mastery, becoming strong, competent and capable.	Confident Noble Brave Focused				
Explorer/ Adventurer/ Pilgrim	Leadership, success, authority, power, control.	Dignified Affirmative Authoritative Future-focused				
Insurgent/ Outlaw	Resisting that which is not helpful, anti-status quo, freedom fighter, extensive turnabout.	Disruptive Individualistic Doer Committed				
Jester	Enjoyment of life, living in the moment. Alternative viewpoints.	Different Carefree Surreal				

S.U.I.T.S.™ Personal Brand Experience

Archetype Names	The archetype's narrative	The archetype's key words	Proof		Connection	
			Visual *(images that you would use to reflect your brand would show…)*	Data *(examples of words that you would use to evoke this archetype in your personal brand communication…)*	Emotive *(what your audience would feel)*	Valuative *(how this meets your audience's needs)*
Guardian/ Protector	Refuge, safety and counsel. Overseer and guidance, self-sacrificing.	Systematic Organised Loyal Caretaker				
Partner/ Confidant/ Everyman	Journeying together. Friendship, standing side-by-side, concerned with your well-being.	Trustworthy Encouraging Compassionate Devout				
Sage/ Mentor/	Insight due to knowledge and understanding. Vision. Making sense.	Judicious Experienced Enquirer Mastery				
Lover	Experiencing pleasure. Requited love. Magnetic.	Enchanting Sensual Sympathetic Mysterious				
The Innocent	Concerned with what is right, optimistic and enthusiastic. Straightforward.	Simplicity Wholesome Happy Honest				

▲ *Table Nineteen: Personal Brand Experience*

PART 2 As you would a piece of milky, unpolished carbon, ready to express its dazzle, you can now cut and polish as many pieces of archetypes as you need to gain the best yield.

A) Create the unique archetype blend for your personal brand by showing how the three archetypes overlay one another and the percentage overlap.

B) Provide words, phrases that would describe the character trait where the archetypes overlapped.

C) Now define the essence where the three circles overlap.
Use 5–7 key words to describe the essence and then create a narrative – write a story.

D) Give the new archetype blend a name to uniquely personify your Personal Brand Master Archetype.

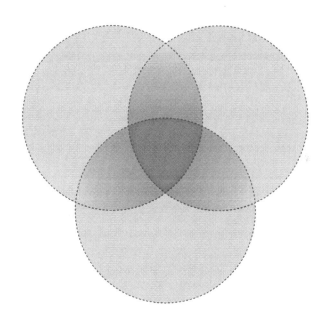

▲ *Diagram Seven: S.U.I.T.S.™ Personal Brand Archetype Master*

PART 3 With your unique master archetype constructed, adapt it for each product/service, keeping alignment with your master archetype. Give each expression a name that best represents the blend. This will enable you to hold on to your authenticity and integrity while adapting for the specific need in the market.

S.U.I.T.S.™ *Personal Brand Archetype Blend – Part 3*			
Product Description	Percentage of Archetype 1	Percentage of Archetype 2	Percentage of Archetype 3	Archetype Blend Name
Service Description	Percentage of Archetype 1	Percentage of Archetype 2	Percentage of Archetype 3	Archetype Blend Name

▲ *Table Nineteen: Personal Brand Product and Service Archetype Blend*

Knowing that the whole is greater than the sum of the parts and that you are not trapped in a way of being, thinking, doing, or acting, what stops you from embracing yourself? What do you need to let go of?

How will this support the person you could be, become, do – where could you go?

> *"If a man has no tea in him, he is incapable of understanding truth and beauty".*
>
> **– Japanese proverb –**

Collective Consciousness is Culture

Culture is how you cultivate shared values, beliefs, and attitudes between your audience and yourself. It is how you set up and interact in relationships. In your personal brand expression, you will experience culture intellectually and demonstrate it physically. It will become the collective awareness within which you celebrate life and serve others – expressing your brand and developing real estate in the mind of your consumer.

Your culture is an essential component of what would ultimately contribute to your personal brand success.

You invested the past chapters in creating the components of this framework; chiselling your purpose, deciding what was really important for you, how to grow, what characteristics and behaviours would benefit you and accelerate your performance, how to express them, and how you fit into your audience's world.

Because culture, by definition, affects performance, having a clear understanding of the type of culture you want to create assists greatly in achieving what you set out to do. An agile culture leads your audience to feel like they are part of you as they gain satisfaction from the contribution you make to their success.

What is an agile culture?

In 2001, a band of software developers created the Agile Manifesto. The purpose of the gambit was to summarise a better way of approaching software development projects. The manifesto pointed out the following:

"We value:
• Individuals and interactions over processes and tools;
• Customer collaboration over contract negotiation;
• Working software over comprehensive documentation;
• Responding to change over following a plan" [33].

I have seen this thinking in action, both in software and in projects. And each time it has been refreshing and energising.

There are 12 key principles in the manifesto. I find the following to be the most helpful in crafting a strategy for your culture: "Develop small, incremental releases and iterate AND focus on frequent delivery of products/services" [34].

This translates into personal branding speak as follows: "Develop and deploy incremental releases of your culture framework as you learn from your audience through feedback, frequently delivering an enhancement of your previous interaction, thereby continuously improving your cultural experience as you establish your brand."

What is an agile culture? One that has a clear goal, gets there through collaboration and cooperation takes small sprints towards achieving the goal, and reviews its impact and performance often in order to learn from and improve the experience.

The Culture grid that I created is founded on agile thinking. The rows indicate the type of culture that is available within the S.U.I.T.S.™ framework – your audience's experience of your personal brand. You may want to add other components. In the columns, I have placed three modes of expressing your vocation. You may want to create other modes you can deliver.

	Support	Enable	Lead
Master	Responsive to challenges, empowers people, promotes initiative. Leader in service	Creates cross functionality, provides frameworks, diminishes boundaries, promotes relationships. Leader in shift	Confident in the future, global mindset, creates trends, promotes breakthrough. Leader in potential
	Stimulate	**Innovate**	**Council**
Specialist	Create opportunities, experimentation, promotes change. Leader in process	Welcomes diversity, rewards curiousness, promotes impact. Leader in energy	Holds and supports trust, provides value and insight, provides connection. Leader in Communication
	Train	**Compete**	**Win**
Generalist	Improves productivity, evaluative, promotes efficiency. Leader in product	Entrepreneurship cultivated, tests the status quo, promotes speed of decisioneering. Leader in boldness	Benchmarking the best, confidence in direction, expert and competent. Promotes performance. Leader in strength
	Transactional	***Transformational***	***Transworth***

▲ *Table Twenty-one: S.U.I.T.S.™ Personal Brand Culture Grid*

✺ *TAILOR YOUR BRAND: PERSONAL BRAND CULTURE*

Consider your living artefacts and review the extent to which they comply with the agile approach. Do the necessary enhancements. Does your manifesto still make sense? Is your project charter up to date? How's your change model compliant with the work you have done?

From the provided culture grid, choose one manifesto or a combination of manifestos to outline the way in which you will interact with your audience, how you will compile your communication, and how you will honour your values for the work you are doing in Timmulation.

> *"When we buy a stake in the future, what we're actually buying is how it makes us feel today".*
>
> **– Seth Godin, It's almost impossible to sell the future –**

Time for a new wardrobe?

A Danish author, Hans Christian Andersen, wrote a fable of two suitmakers. "The Emperor's new clothes" promised to be a fraud gauge. Subjects of the emperor who were unfit for their positions, simple, or incompetent, would not be able to see the flattering outfit. This promised to be an elegant and powerful solution that would imbue the wearer with confidence and prominence whilst cleaning up Parliament.

Ultimately, a child blurted out, "But he isn't wearing anything at all!" And that turned out to be the simple truth. The lesson here is that your packaging is as important as your content - specifically others' perception of it is more important than your opinion on the matter.

To get the perfect fit of a suit that represents you, you would need to work with a tailor whom you could bounce your ideas off, and he/she would advise you if you were only wearing your birthday suit. Ideally there should be a third party whom you trust to give you this type of honest feedback.

There are many considerations that ultimately render a product perfect.

Combined, in this S.U.I.T.S.™ project, your physical presence and your being (mind, thoughts) constitute the product. The packaging is how you show up – your behaviour.

It is true that, for many consumers, the product and the package are one and the same thing. Often, your audience makes purchasing decisions based on the perceptions that it develops during and after the evaluation of the offer. The audience uses its sensory highways for input and makes the decision based on what it is experiencing on that day. It seldom buys a stake in the future. Will the way you plan to show up communicate your value?

Package design, therefore, adds value to the product and provides the audience with a visual connection - the sensory system that is the default information stream for the majority of audience members. The purpose of the design is to attract attention and communicate value: perhaps not the kind of attention that the protagonist in the Emperor's fable experienced. Good packaging sets you apart and differentiates you from your competitors.

In personal branding, you have the opportunity to craft a) your image, b) the environment within which you operate, and c) the items that touch your expression.

➡ **A) Your image comprises elements such as**

The multifaceted expression in your wardrobe – formal, casual, business, etc.;

Personal presentation i.e., hairstyle, skin quality, physique;

Accessories i.e., writing instruments, jewellery, mode of transport etc.

➡ **B) The environment within which you operate includes**

The space that you call your own: your home and office interiors;

The venues where you interact: recreational venues and activities, restaurants you frequent, places where you holiday, etc.;

The friends you keep, your business network.

➡ **C) The items that present expressions of you include**

Your habits and hobbies;

The books you read, the conversations you have, the statements you make on social media, etc.

The truth is, people will draw conclusions based on what is happening to them and the brands you associate with. They will form perceptions of you, ultimately making their purchasing decisions based on a blend of what you put forward and what they filter through their perceptions.

> • How are you the same as the brands that your audience already interacts with – red ocean? How are you different – blue ocean [g]?
> • What value will they get from 'buying' you?

Here is where you leverage the value of stereotypes and, by association, borrow the credibility that other brands have in the mind's eye and experience of your audience.

❋ *TAILOR YOUR BRAND: PACKAGE DESIGN GUIDELINES*

In the package design, the following is a high-level view of the elements from which you will benefit from when you consider designing your packaging and expressing your identity. Create a packaging checklist of the items that represent you. Conduct an audit of the current state of affairs, and populate the corresponding actions into your living artefacts.

PART 1 What is the tone of your voice – leading on from the archetype exercise, what words, written and spoken communication, best align with what you're offering? What language is inappropriate? How does your language capture the heart of your audience?

PART 2 What is your slogan – that short, striking and memorable phrase, leading on from the promises that you made. Your slogan would do well to clearly articulate the healing benefits of your brand. I find the following seven statements a helpful starting point from which you can articulate and craft your promise into a healing benefit for your audience:

- You are a Visionary: seeing and designing the future – healing hopelessness
- You are an Attaché: liaising and establishing command – healing injustice
- You are a Guru: instructing best practice – healing helplessness
- You are an Advocate: providing wise counsel and direction – healing discouragement
- You are a Patron: administering resources – healing lack
- You are a Ruler: establishing and empowering liberty – healing 'being stuck'
- You are a Dean: creating satisfaction and facilitating achievement – healing esteem

PART 3 How are you priced? Although this is not a packaging element, it is a factor that contributes to packaging. How does the perceived value that you bring align with the pricing that you've selected?

PART 4 Being clear on the features (that which you do well) as a human being in the context of the product (your personal brand) is vital to your packaging. Having these features communicated clearly as part of your packaging strategy is pivotal for your audience's experience understanding your value in an appropriate form. Here is a list of key qualities that create success in the current economy and the new virtual economy of this millennium. Consider the list and rate yourself on the scale for each item.

- Interpersonal skill: Generally, this refers to the life skill of being able to communicate and interact with others as individuals, teams, and groups. It is resourceful for establishing strong relationships and achieving one another's mutual intent. It relates to your emotional intelligence and how you cluster your traits, fit for purpose.
- Assertiveness: It is linked to self-esteem and is defined as the quality of being self-assured and confident without being aggressive. It is how you behave when you are taking a stand or making a statement. Assertiveness is the affirmation of your right to a point of view and your ability to hold that point of view without being threatening or assuming dominance over others.

- Effective communication: the combination of a set of skills that includes verbal and non-verbal communication, managing what is happening to you at the present moment, displaying engaged listening, the capacity to recognise that communication is a two-way street between parties. The perception that you have been understood and heard is a measure of success.

- Tough conversations: This is the upgrade of effective communication. The stakes are high and failure comes at a real cost. This feature is tricky as the emotional intelligence component outweighs the content of the conversation and the content of the conversation is the reason for its stickiness.

- Being approachable: It is the sense that you are easy to interact with. This social skill encourages dialogue and conversations by virtue of your relevance in your environment.

Review the packaging guidelines and develop your requirements for engaging training, coaching, mentoring, and consultation to amplify the above qualities

The packaging should also clearly communicate what benefits the customer/audience will experience. The following is not an exhaustive list but an indication of what I have found to be important for a business and its consumers:

- Accessing Creativity: It is about offering fresh awareness with discernment, resulting in insight as you work your way towards a breakthrough – it can be seen as the energy that leads to innovation.

- Innovation: you can translate ideas into value, either as a product, a service, the forging of an alliance or the consolidation/ establishment/creation of a process. It involves the deliberate merging of a requirement through the imagination to derive an intuitive result that is useful to the business and its consumer.

- Initiative: This is about enthusiasm to engage in an action to achieve the stated intent.

- Driving for results: Harnesses energy to improve performance and the way things are done.

- Problem solving: This is about solutions. It entails finding the essence of the challenge, internal or external, and supporting those who are involved

- Making decisions: This is the application of problem-solving as it involves the choice of a course of action. It includes creating a constructive environment, understanding the circumstances clearly, offering alternatives, exploring options, and committing to the most resourceful plan as you communicate the way forward.
- Delegating and duplicating: is about offering people whom you trust the opportunity to deliver on specific outcomes where there is clear understanding of controls and limitations and sufficient support from you. A key component of successfully duplicating yourself is giving recognition where it is due.
- Political Acuity: Involves astuteness regarding the long and short game with the players involved knowing how to approach the situation and when to act.

Use Table Twenty-two and populate the additional four areas as they align with your goals and ultimate objective.

In summary – Chapter Five

Power to you – the owner of your choices and the designer of how you do you.

You are not a victim or stuck by fate to your future.

You have the power and the unique authority to solve the challenges that your world is facing right now.

Stereotypes can serve a positive purpose, and using archetypes of common experiences fast-tracks your brand engagement

Packaging plays a key role in the decision-making.

Creating a culture through which your audience can interact with you and that you can build into becomes a Golden Circle of touchpoints.

What is in the next chapter?

You will explore how to create:

- An Iconic Branding framework to achieve your brand leadership status
- An Engagement strategy for your Personal Brand to captivate your audience levels. ⓦ

S.U.I.T.S.™ Personal Brand Tactical Plan

THEME: (from SOW) — **OBJECTIVE:** (from Charter) — **Cycle Dates:**

GOAL 1: (from Charter)		GOAL 2: (from Charter)		GOAL 3: (from Charter)	
Activities/ Daily Actions	Time Milestones	Activities/ Daily Actions	Time Milestones	Activities/ Daily Actions	Time Milestones
Sensory Systems to activate/utilise	Values to activate/ draw on	Sensory Systems to activate/utilise	Values to activate/ draw on	Sensory Systems to activate/utilise	Values to activate/ draw on
Energy Zones to activate/utilise	Motivational ladder to activate/utilise	Energy Zones to activate/utilise	Motivational ladder to activate/utilise	Energy Zones to activate/utilise	Motivational ladder to activate/utilise
Tools that I can use	RASCI (who to involve)	Tools that I can use	RASCI (who to involve)	Tools that I can use	RASCI (who to involve)
Target Market	Product Service match	Target Market	Product Service match	Target Market	Product Service match
Brand Archetype blend	Culture Focus	Brand Archetype blend	Culture Focus	Brand Archetype blend	Culture Focus
Key Packaging considerations	Communicate Benefits and Features	Key Packaging considerations	Communicate Benefits and Features	Key Packaging considerations	Communicate Benefits and Features
Income I am expecting	Investment I need to incur	Income I am expecting	Investment I need to incur	Income I am expecting	Investment I need to incur

▲ Table Twenty-two: S.U.I.T.S.™ Personal Brand Tactical Plan v3

MATT WHITE

TIMMULATION

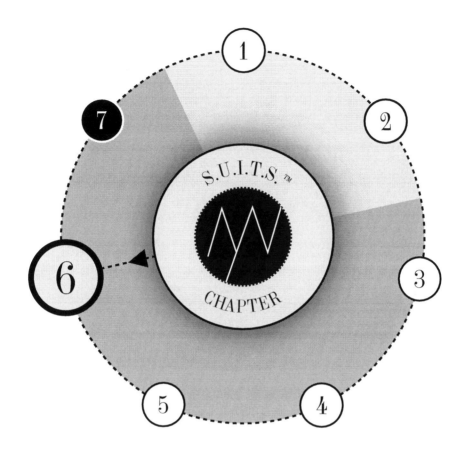

MATT WHITE

CHAPTER SIX

Activate it – Timmulation: A communication expression through the stimulation of time

Your fourth portmanteau is Timmulation: "the process of indefinite interactions amongst entities during the progress of time as shaped by tangible and intangible tools".

Hanging in our lounge all through the years of my childhood was a small-scale copy of a masterpiece by Rembrandt van Rijn. I came across the painting again in the history of art class when I was sixteen. I was an apprentice manning a slide show. I found myself in the presence of the Master most recently on my last trip to Amsterdam.

Nothing could prepare me for the encounter I had in the Rijksmuseum.

The Night Watch's (Dutch: De Nachtwacht) sheer size is intimidating. It measures 3,630 mm × 4,370 mm (11.91 ft × 14.34 ft) and with chiaroscuro, the effective use of light and shadow, the painting mesmerised me.

> *"Live as if you were living a second time, and as though you had acted wrongly the first time".*
>
> **– Victor Frankle –**

I sat in front of the painting for what seemed like hours.

When you go deeper into the meaning of the painting you'll find that it is symmetrically divided to illustrate the union of the Dutch Protestants and the Dutch Catholics whilst simultaneously invoking the war effort against the Spaniards. It seems that the management and elegant representation of ambiguity and paradox is an ancient art.

With the composition and the persuasive use of colour, your eyes are directed to three characters in the crowd; the two gentlemen in the centre, from whom the painting gets its full title: The Shooting Company of Frans Banning Cocq and Willem van Ruytenburch. The girl in the centre-left background (behind them) is a type of mascot. The artist successfully displayed the traditional emblems of the arquebusiers (Dutch for hook-gun brigade) by weaving various elements into the story. They include the claws of a dead chicken, a pistol which represents a clover, the militia's goblet, a helmet with an oak leaf, and the ample use of the colour yellow, which is often associated with victory.

The captain of the voluntary city guard, Captain Banning Cocq, and 17 of his regiment members commissioned De Nachtwacht although 18 members appear on the shield in the background, because the drummer got in for free (as drummers do).

Legend has it that Marie de Medici, the Queen of France, went into exile in 1638 (on the order of her son, Louis XVIII, another brute). She was received in the Musketeers' Meeting Hall in Amsterdam with great fanfare: The painting was first hung and unveiled upon her arrival. We know that the painting was completed in 1642, the peak of the Dutch Golden Age – what are you learning about legends and stories as they relate to your personal brand?

The Night Watch continued to inspire across the ages. Examples include musical works such as the second movement of Gustav Mahler's 7th Symphony, in Nightwatching, a film by director Peter Greenaway (that suggests that Rembrandt may have immortalised a conspiracy theory), and in the literature of Agustina Bessa Luís (A Ronda da Noite).

The Night Watch is important in the context of personal branding as it illustrates the significance of going the extra M.I.L.E®. More about the M.I.L.E® in chapter 7. The genius of The Night Watch also captures the principles of iconic branding:

- Find (create) the ideal conditions for your identity (brand).
- Create and be the story others want to be part of.
- Interrupt the way things are.
- Imbue your brand with your signature.
- Innovate – be the first.
- Leverage PR – make the most of your airtime and what others are saying about you.
- Maintain your brand through relationships (marketing) and communication (advertising).

My high school (college) teacher remarked, "Having prints of good art adorning your walls is much better than having originals of poor art". This confirmed to me that my mother knew what she was doing when she educated her two brutes in culture.

Like the Night Watch, the richness of your brand experience will enjoy the influence of colour, texture, composition, message, location, and association. Moreover, it could ultimately have a timeless impact on the present generations and on those to come.

In the preface to this book you created a state which you are now going to use in this section. This exercise is similar to what you did in the other chapters. What was that state? Is it still the most resourceful state for you to use? Can you fully access it now? Is it everything that you are now aware of? How do you rate your iconic leadership ability?

✹ TAILOR YOUR BRAND: ICONIC BRANDING FRAMEWORK

Use the following table to create the Iconic Brand Framework for your personal brand encounters.

	What condition must I create?	What success story do they want to be part of?	How will I effectively interrupt their world?	What part of my signature will this touchpoint hold?	With what am I the first?
Sacred Glyph: Functional Level					
Sacred Glyph: Experiential Level					
Sacred Glyph: Symbolic Level					
Sacred Glyph: Metaphysical Level					

▲ *Table Twenty-three: Iconic Branding Framework*

Keeping Your Promise in the Context of Iconic Leadership

Political acuity in this age of leadership may well be the secret code to pleasing the demanding lordship of expectations. The delivery of promises made when there were minor setbacks and major fortunes would baffle any aspiring monarch in training. To achieve Iconic Leadership, you will be required to inspire faith and provide proof that you are a leader worth following.

One of the ancient Hebrew kings said, "There is an appointed time for everything, for every delight and event and purpose under heaven" [35].

Timing is everything. I concur.

The Hersey-Blanchard Situational Leadership Model [36] agrees. It states that there are five ways to engage in situations: telling, selling, participating, delegating and being able to know when you need to carry out the essence of Iconic Leadership in delivery through clarity.

With the help of the S.U.I.T.S.™ model, you crafted a project charter outlining the vision for your personal brand. The project charter provides you with a guideline for the key performance indicators and your tactical plan is your way of ensuring that you're delivering the vision on a day-to-day basis. Fundamentally, the change model that you have will be affected to ensure that the change necessary to deliver your vision is implemented smoothly and thoroughly as you rally the support of others for your highest intent.

Choosing a SUIT

When stitching your personal brand together, you were challenged with decisions: great ones, small ones, significant ones, and obvious ones. Sometimes you will find yourself stumped, not knowing how to make a decision. My indecision normally concerns the consequences for the impacted relationships. So, when I cannot count on my mental, cognitive, or emotional skills, I revert to a scorecard.

I have created my Personal Brand Decisioneering Scorecard over three decades and it has seen many iterations. They include an elaborate point system, a software-based decision matrix, and a simple and elegant statement: "Will the result of (the decision that I need to make), create, foster and advance my experience of faith, hope, love, and joy and will it give me peace?" The answer is the decision that I will make, and to date, this equation has not failed me.

The important thing about knowing how to make a decision concerns how it enables your engagement strategy. Your audience is buying products and services based on what is happening to its members now. Throughout the book, you created an authentic and integrated personal brand. The next section partners that with packaging in that it creates the opportunity to connect with your audience in the moment and convert its members into brand advocates.

PART 1 Use the table for touch-point engagement strategy and consider the following questions:

	What does the audience need most right now	What is the message I need to craft to connect with them around this need (one liner)	What blend of three channels is best aligned for the audience to receive this message	When does my audience connect with the message in a meaningful way to make decisions about engaging my brand	How will I measure the success of the touchpoint?
Sacred Glyph: Functional Level	e.g. consider themes such as: urgency, innovation, limited availability, legacy alignment, quick wins	e.g. consider themes such as: urgency, innovation, limited availability, legacy alignment, quick wins	e.g. SMS, WhatsApp Chat, LinkedIn, Pinterest, Instagram, Facebook, YouTube, Blog, Conference, Print Media	e.g. Monday morning at 10am before the management meeting	e.g. When I follow up with a phone call on Tuesday at 8am and my customer takes my call and I secure an appointment
Sacred Glyph: Experiential Level					
Sacred Glyph: Symbolic Level					
Sacred Glyph: Metaphysical Level					

▲ *Table Twenty-four: S.U.I.T.S. ™ Engagement Strategy*

Once you have created your encounter framework and the engagement strategy, populate your personal brand tactical plan v4 (the following table) by matching your 28-day focus to your audience and what you want to achieve at the next milestone.

PART 2 Use the Personal Brand Artefact Audit Table and consider the tools you need to create to provide the necessary artefacts for your Personal Brand – the table is not exhaustive; it is merely an indication of what may be required – please enrich as needed.

Electronic Touch points:	Electronic Stationery:	Physical Touch Points:
Personal Website incl. Blog, Professional Facebook Page, Professional Instagram Page, Personal LinkedIn Profile, Business LinkedIn Profile	(PPT template, letterhead, email signature profile, updated and relevant CV, etc.)	(Business Cards, Presentation folder, Letterhead, Product & Service brochures, Published Intellectual Property, etc.)

The items that you need so that you can brief the technical and creative support teams to create the above artefacts, summarised in a presentation, include your statement of work, sacred glyph, relationship matrix, products and services with benefits, culture grid, archetype blend, and your most recent tactical plan.

S.U.I.T.S. ™ Personal Brand Tactical Plan

THEME: (from SOW)	OBJECTIVE: (from Charter)	Cycle Dates:

GOAL 1: (from Charter)		GOAL 2: (from Charter)		GOAL 3: (from Charter)	
Activities/ Daily Actions	Time Milestones	Activities/ Daily Actions	Time Milestones	Activities/ Daily Actions	Time Milestones
Sensory Systems to activate/utilise	Values to activate/ draw on	Sensory Systems to activate/utilise	Values to activate/ draw on	Sensory Systems to activate/utilise	Values to activate/ draw on
Energy Zones to activate/utilise	Motivational ladder to activate/utilise	Energy Zones to activate/utilise	Motivational ladder to activate/utilise	Energy Zones to activate/utilise	Motivational ladder to activate/utilise
Tools that I can use	RASCI (who to involve)	Tools that I can use	RASCI (who to involve)	Tools that I can use	RASCI (who to involve)
Target Market	Product Service match	Target Market	Product Service match	Target Market	Product Service match
Brand Archetype blend	Culture Focus	Brand Archetype blend	Culture Focus	Brand Archetype blend	Culture Focus
Key Packaging considerations	Communicate Benefits and Features	Key Packaging considerations	Communicate Benefits and Features	Key Packaging considerations	Communicate Benefits and Features
Iconic Brand Focus	Engagement Focus	Iconic Brand Focus	Engagement Focus	Iconic Brand Focus	Engagement Focus
Income I am expecting	Investment I need to incur	Income I am expecting	Investment I need to incur	Income I am expecting	Investment I need to incur

▲ Table Twenty-five: S.U.I.T.S. ™ Personal Brand Tactical Plan v3

In summary - Chapter Six

The timing and the quality of the interactions your audience will have with your brand will lead to the impact of your brand as part of your legacy.

The creation of your Iconic Personal brand is the art and science of distilling your value into a consumable product/service which meets the needs of your audience in time, fit for purpose which comes to life through an engagement strategy

What is in the next chapter?

- Crafting a memorable message which aligns with your brand essence.
- You will learn a technique for writing a brand story for your audience which increases engagement.
- An overview of the market for the next thirty years.
- How to create future-based myths to activate your brand for your audience in the now.
- How to stay anchored to yourself in order to be present for your audience through your brand. 🐾

MATT WHITE

SPLENDANCE

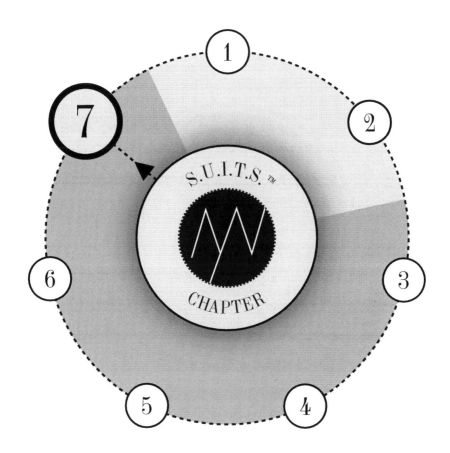

MATT WHITE

CHAPTER SEVEN

Move it — Splendance: The gateway into every day

The last portmanteau in S.U.I.T.S.™ is Splendance: "the elegance of telling a story that unfolds splendour".

Why is splendour an important concept in storytelling? Because splendour is many things – it is the magnificence of an achievement, the sumptuousness of a meal, the grandeur of a ballroom, the impressiveness of a personality, the resplendence of an art piece, the opulence of gifting, the luxury of time, the richness of a relationship, the fineness of sympathy, the lavishness of kindness, the ornateness of design, the glory of a simple life, the beauty of the desert, the elegance of silence, the majesty of the universe, the stateliness of age and the impact of wisdom.

> *"Don't be satisfied with stories, how things have gone with others.*
>
> *Unfold your own myth".*
>
> **– Jalaluddin Rumi –**

And because splendour is many things, you have to smith a message that will unlock the experience of splendance for your audience.

A message of magnificence

Martha Graham said, "I have spent all my life with dance and being a dancer. It's permitting life to use you in a very intense way. Sometimes it is not pleasant. Sometimes it is fearful. But nevertheless, it is inevitable."

What struck me about this quote from the American dancer and choreographer, who invented the language of modern dance, was the inevitability of being used and, implicitly, of being óf use.

Martha used her language to reveal the passion and ecstasy of the human experience, which earned her the right to be the first dancer ever to travel abroad as a cultural ambassador. For her work, she received the highest civilian award an American citizen could obtain, the Medal of Freedom.

I spoke about Olympic medals in the preface of this book. I described the price of hard work but failed to mention the other accolades that deserving individuals could achieve to adorn their purpose through striving. Over a period of 20 years, Martha danced and choreographed her way into receiving the key of the City of Paris and Japan's Imperial Order of the Precious Crown.

Martha liberated the human spirit and body from the restrictions of formal dance (which required years of technical training, for which the reward was entrapment in a stringent and perhaps delusional cult). I challenge you to do the same with your personal brand.

But what good is hard work without a story to tell and people to share the journey with? Your audience can only care about being part of your story when they understand the relevance of the experience in the context of their meaning. To achieve this, we have spent ample time developing your purpose and matching it up to your audience's needs. All that is left is wordsmithery to iron out your message.

As Martha Graham did, you should create a new language that can become a dance and then a movement. You may not consider yourself a worthy dance partner or even a transformational leader, but right now you're your own best bet.

Until boredom us do part

What makes your brand unique, over and above the fact that there is only one of you, is the relationship that you will build as you tell your story and interact with your audience. Think of your message as a multiple season series that, for now, has no end but multiple conclusions along the way. This series has multiple platforms through which your audience can engage: an online platform, multiple books, mass media expression, a movie, etc. Now imagine how your story enthrals your audience and takes it on a journey through the expected and unexpected, teaching its members to love and live with your characters and to look forward to the next episode.

The caveat is this. When the story moves too fast, your audience may lose interest expending too much effort trying to keep up. When it moves too slow, the audience may get bored and change the channel.

What then is the answer to an engaging story?

Nigel Watts's book on "Writing a novel and getting published" presents the Eight-Point Story Arc [h]. It is a failsafe, fool-proof, and time-honoured structure that will enable you to craft your personal brand story into a message as you work on a communications and marketing plan.

The Eight Points of the Story Arc, in order, are as follows; stasis, trigger, the quest, surprise, critical choice, climax, reversal, and resolution. According to Nigel, every classic plot goes through these stages and serves as a framework rather than a set of sequential events. To take you through your messaging, I will explain how the 8 points relate to creating your brand story. A story that cannot have an ending, but has a forever after, a 'then what?'

To establish credibility and association with your audience, the 'I am like you' occurrence, your story needs to start in everyday life, stasis – where you can find yourself and your audience.

Then something happens: something beyond the control of your audience, a trigger, the catalyst that begets the story – the challenge that needs to be answered to seemingly allow life as usual to continue.

This catalyst which is beyond anyone's control results in an experience, something pleasant (getting a promotion) or unpleasant (losing a job), which means that the clock is ticking towards the intensification of the positive experience or the re-establishment of the status quo. At this point, you emphasise the pain that the audience experiences as a result of the trigger or present an inquiry into what other possibilities are available now that the door is unlocked.

Next, the big surprise happens. This can present itself as a combination of enjoyable circumstances and challenging barriers. This is the part of the story where you present your solution. Your answer to the situation should be unexpected but plausible and should have an immediate beneficial experience.

Now your audience faces a crucial decision. Its members need to expose the reality of their lives. These moments of elevated tension offer your audience the opportunity to choose. This means that you should have options available: three or four or five, no more and no less. Two options constitute an ultimatum, not a choice; and more than five options are overwhelming.

Once the audience has made a decision, the climax of the story unfolds – here, depending on the story you've created, you will need to choose a suitable entertaining experience according to the options that were on the table.

The reversal part of the story is about how the state and status of the character change. Here, you imply the action that your audience should be able to take as a result of your brand association and the consumption of your products and/or services. The reversal of your story should both be likely and certain. The reality is that, for every action, there is a reaction. Therefore, the state of change can't fall out of the sky but has to be a relentless unfolding of events leading to the resolution.

And so, stasis returns, new, different, wiser, and liberated. Although the resolution is the conclusion of the story, it could very well be the beginning of another. For more illustrations or thoughts on the matter of writing stories, get hold of "Writing a Novel".

Dropping into the middle of a story

The largest occurrence in Western history is currently taking place in the market, and you are right in the middle of it. A workforce and an audience that will dominate the next 30 years on the planet is rising like Jupiter over Mars.

Not only will this mass of people be the most educated generation in Western history, but it also finds its women leading as they pursue tougher academic programs and participate in more advanced strategies for business than their male counterparts.

How will your story accommodate and be relevant to an informed and technologically savvy audience?

These digital natives are mobile and keep themselves entertained and on the cutting edge. They stay abreast through their social profiles. The impact of this mindset is that this audience believes that technology should allow people to use their time more efficiently and should drive connectedness. The audience's awareness of the global and local community supports its greater focus on society's needs than on its own needs. It expects government to address society's biggest issues and will hold it accountable for the rising equality gap. Items on the agenda for this audience include free trade, consumer protection, and regulation – essentially, whatever happens must be fair according to them. They are a compassionate generation.

This mass of people is conscious that driving the interests of all stakeholders will increase the expectation that organised business will amplify its social responsibility and environmental accountability. In addition, this audience has the mindset that it can influence the world through the power of its wallet and is not scared to use it.

Although this might be the biggest story in Western history, your audience members think of themselves as global citizens transcending and embracing diversity. They are outraged by social injustice and are willing to take action to make the world a more equitable and sustainable place. Imagine them enrolled in the school of entrepreneurship. They have managed to graduate from the recession of 2008 and have changed their career expectations as they are subscribing members of the Economy of Self.

Imagine being part of a civilisation that believes in creating its own luck, working on projects rather than careers. Starting and failing is a way of life and success is almost not the point, but comfort is. In addition to this ideal world, the civilisation is pragmatic about bringing about change, which is evident in its mantras, "Believe in your dreams" and "You can make it happen".

In contrast to its liberal attitude, this new wave of people supports conservative economic policies and alternative medicine. These liberals are the answer to socio-political challenges as they volunteer to help others, expressing disdain for selfishness.

Challenging the system because there is something which can be improved on is their everyday stance. This is the result of their independent thinking and disbelief in the mass media. The maverick move that this new wave of people will need to undertake entails progressiveness for the sake of progress. With their embrace of innovation and new ideas, I wonder how you will create boundaries that they will find resourceful and feel comfortable in.

This tsunami of hopeful and confident people is approaching your shores. I trust that you have embraced the fact that they will expect you to achieve the impossible. Those are the expectations they have of themselves.

They will also expect processes and services to work fast as they have little to no tolerance for unreliability and lack of value. All-encompassing diversity (including race, gender, sexuality, heritage, culture, and religion) is the trademark of this open-minded wave. They prioritize collaboration over division, teamwork over self-achievement, and cause over capital.

Technology offers the people that belong to this swell the ability to do more things at the same time. Hence, research on multitasking may need to be updated due to the influence of technology after all. It seems that negative pressure fires their nomadic existence; not only do they cross physical boundaries, but they also live outside restrictive norms. With the Fourth Industrial Revolution in full swing, communication from anywhere to anywhere all the time enables their wanderlust and independence from geography and time. Products and services which offer answers to the insatiable impatience of this adventurous mass of people and package danger with excitement will make a memorable impact on their new way of existence.

The extra M.I.L.E.®
(mythical, imaginative, loyalty, emotion)

People remember and retell stories that connect with a deep emotion regarding something that truly matters to them. Consider the story from Greek mythology: King Odysseus of Ithaca, the man behind the design of the Trojan horse – a strategic move on an impenetrable city. The myth of the Trojan horse and the love of Paris for Helen is well told. This story holds together the four pillars of going the extra mile in crafting brand communication. It is memorable and is central to the myth, activates the imagination, illustrates loyalty and brings about the energy which results in deep emotions – like love, injustice, desire, brotherhood, sacrifice etc. – result in.

When you connect – keep it R.E.A.L.®
(Ritual, Empower, Artistry, Liberate)

I have four bastions that I recommend you adopt until you create anchors that will enable you to simultaneously be in the moment and serve your audience in the future. The purpose of having four pillars is to enrich your brand experience in the context of the story in the marketplace for the next 30 years.

The purpose of the first bastion is to create a ritual that comprises a series of actions or types of behaviour that you regularly and almost invariably engage in. This can take on any form (from a real-time online chat room every first Tuesday of the month to an annual fundraiser for the local actions of an organisation which works with children). The only requirement is that it aligns with your brand objectives and achieves the purpose of connecting with your audience. Think about how this ritual could enable two-way dialogue and support taking achievement the extra M.I.L.E.®

The second bastion is about the result of the ritual, a.k.a. empowerment. I heard a story about how a family used a ritual technique to empower the young ones in the house. When the children were ready to be taken off the dummy the parents attached it to the string of a helium filled balloon and shared how a child in a faraway land needed the dummy. At the opportune moment, the child released the balloon and the helium angel floated off into the sky. When the child later enquired about the dummy, the parents would remind him/her of the balloon and the other baby. That gave them another opportunity to connect with the child regarding life and helping others. The purpose of connecting with your audience through a ritual is to leave them empowered by the value that you add to their lives (through your engagement and not your sales pitch).

The Japanese have an art form known as Kintsugi which undertakes to repair broken items with lacquer, dusted or mixed with powdered gold, silver, or platinum. The Japanese philosophy states that the breakage and repair of the broken object is part of its history and expresses mushin – 'no mind'. It advocates for non-attachment, the acceptance of change and fate as aspects of human life. It may even be that the value of the object increases in its broken state, and it is therefore something to celebrate rather than disguise. In the work that I do, Artistry – the third bastion, has many different expressions – from the elegance in a coaching technique to the composition of an interior or the strategy of a brand. How will you access artistry for your audience?

Earlier in S.U.I.T.S.™, I referred to Alvin Toffler and his take on the illiterate of the 21st century. The last bastion of connection concerns liberation. How will you assist through your brand's expression of products and services that allows your audience to "learn, unlearn, and relearn" as you offer its members freedom from the captivity of a state that does not enable a future.

In summary – Chapter Seven

Part of your brand's 'je ne sais quoi' quality is creating multiple experiences for your audience to encounter splendour.

The next thirty years in business will be known for the free flow of information, strong connectivity and immediate feedback in consumer cycles and employee engagement.

The people of the future are looking for R.E.A.L. engagement and will keep you accountable as you evoke their patronage.

The current economy that already includes the 'future' provides your brand ample opportunities to connect and engage with your audience, showcasing your artistry as you create a mythical and imaginative world to which your audience will want to be loyal. ⓦ

	What 'mythical' power can you unlock in your brand experience for your audience?	What can you image and communicate with your audience that has never been done before?	How will your audience experience your loyalty?	What deep emotion are you connecting your brand to? How does that inspire your audience?
Sacred Glyph: Functional Level				
Sacred Glyph: Experiential Level				
Sacred Glyph: Symbolic Level				
Sacred Glyph: Metaphysical Level				

▲ *Table Twenty-six: S.U.I.T.S.™ Personal Brand M.I.L.E.® Chart*

S.U.I.T.S.™ Personal Brand Tactical Plan

THEME: (from SOW)	*OBJECTIVE:* (from Charter)	*Cycle Dates:*
GOAL 1: (from Charter)	**GOAL 2:** (from Charter)	**GOAL 3:** (from Charter)
Activities/ Daily Actions	Activities/ Daily Actions	Activities/ Daily Actions
Sensory Systems to activate/utilise	Sensory Systems to activate/utilise	Sensory Systems to activate/utilise
Energy Zones to activate/utilise	Energy Zones to activate/utilise	Energy Zones to activate/utilise
Motivational ladder to activate/utilise	Motivational ladder to activate/utilise	Motivational ladder to activate/utilise
Tools that I can use	Tools that I can use	Tools that I can use
RASCI (who to involve)	RASCI (who to involve)	RASCI (who to involve)
Target Market	Target Market	Target Market
Product Service match	Product Service match	Product Service match
Brand Archetype blend	Brand Archetype blend	Brand Archetype blend
Culture Focus	Culture Focus	Culture Focus
Key Packaging considerations	Key Packaging considerations	Key Packaging considerations
Communicate Benefits and Features	Communicate Benefits and Features	Communicate Benefits and Features
Iconic Brand Focus	Iconic Brand Focus	Iconic Brand Focus
Engagement Focus	Engagement Focus	Engagement Focus
M.I.L.E.™ Focus: L & E	M.I.L.E.™ Focus: M & I	M.I.L.E.™ Focus: M & I
M.I.L.E.™ Focus: M & I	M.I.L.E.™ Focus: L & E	M.I.L.E.™ Focus: L & E
Income I am expecting	Income I am expecting	Income I am expecting
Investment I need to incur	Investment I need to incur	Investment I need to incur

▲ *Table Twenty-seven: S.U.I.T.S.™ Personal Brand Tactical Plan Final*

MATT WHITE

MATT WHITE

FINAL REMARKS

Beyond-you-nique

Often, a sage will ask a question that brings me to a standstill during a coaching conversation:

"What then?"

When I've achieved this goal, when I've obtained that outcome, when I've settled this relationship, when I've landed that job, what then?

Beyond-you-nique is my UVP – ultimate value proposition, my slogan, if you will. It is the answer to that question.

Beyond-you-nique implies that there is something beyond being me and being unique, beyond even the sum of those parts, and it implies a future of worth and the possibilities of destiny.

For me it encapsulates the eternal, the sacred, the precious, the divine, and the timelessness that is the essence of my spirit and the unspoken need of each person I work with.

It is a statement on which I base foundational decisions and with which I challenge my clients. I trust that Beyond-you-nique instils in you the gravitas of the truth that you are, and always will be, so much more than your personal brand and that I will be there to support you in the ways that I can.

I am proud of you. You have shown courage, commitment, and endurance. You have shown me that you are limitless and willing to embrace it. I celebrate your life with you and trust you with the knowledge that that which lies ahead will be everything you need it to be. Until we meet again, I leave you with this Old Irish Blessing. 🌀

May the road rise up to meet you.
May the wind be always at your back.
May the sun shine warm upon your face;
the rains fall soft upon your fields.
And until we meet again,
May God hold you in the palm of His hand.

– Anon –

MATT WHITE

ACKNOWLEDGEMENTS

I am thankful for my willing early readers.

Moreover, I am blessed to have the enthusiasm of avid supporters, Vanessa Boshoff, Tony Davis, Michael Healy, and Robin Pullen.

For the cardinal and godly intervention of Leola Anthony and Bill Price in my life and for their courage and forbearance with me, I am grateful.

I thank Elize Ferner for her unmistakable valuable first stab at the editing.

My coaches, Tim Goodenough, Rob Smale, Rob Labushagné, Zi Hattingh, Mark Holsthauzen, Reinhard Korb, and Waldo van Heereden offered many valuable insights.

For my superb crew, Luke Palder (Proofreading Services), Hesti Steenkamp (Designer), Aaron Matthews (Web Guy), Christy Nailand (Web Girl), Shaun Victor (Digital and PR) who got the job done and the word onto the street, you are all sensational.

I thank Kgomotso Sekhute and Koketso Manstane, the PENOLOGIC business bastion of strength for allowing me to lean so heavily on them for support.

And I thank Elsabé Breytenbach and Lourens Terblanche for allowing me to be home.

Wilhelm, Marti and Tys, who have had my back for decades and change: Thank you, and I love you.

I am also compelled to thank readers, booksellers, and librarians for embracing S.U.I.T.S.™ the way they have.

I am humbled by all your contributions. ⬤

MATT WHITE

NOTES AND REFERENCES

1. See the work of the psychologist, Csikszentmihalyi, on "Flow".

2. See International Society of Neuro-Semantics at
   www.neurosemantics.com

3. Author unknown

4. Simon Sinek, *https://www.startwithwhy.com*

5. *http://www.neurosemantics.com/michael-hall/*

6. Doran, G. T. (1981). "There's a S.M.A.R.T. way to write management's goals
   and objectives". Management Review. AMA FORUM. 70 (11): 35–36.

7. The Business Case Template is adapted from Buttrick, The Project
   Workout, p. 287.

8. Prosci's research-based methodology
   https://www.prosci.com/change-management/thought-leadership-library/
   integrated-individual-and-organizational-cm-methodology

9. *https://www.prosci.com/adkar/adkar-model*

10. The Holy Bible, Proverbs 23:7

11. *http://madagascar.dreamworks.com*

12. Engaging the Neural Matrix, Ian Weinberg, 2013.

13. A Theory of Human Motivation, A. H. Maslow (1943), Originally Published
    in Psychological Review, 50, 370-396.

14. Hormones and Behavior; The reactive scope model – A new model
    integrating homeostasis, allostasis, and stress; L. Michael Romero, Molly J.
    Dickens, Nicole E. Cyr, Department of Biology, Tufts University, Medford,
    USA, © 2008 Elsevier Inc.

15. Secrets of Personal Mastery, L. Michael Hall, Ph.D., 2009, Crownhouse
    Publishing, p15

16. Seligman, Martin E. P. Authentic Happiness: Using the New Positive
    Psychology to Realize Your Potential for Lasting Fulfillment. New York:
    The Free Press, 2002.

17. Trauma and the Body: A Sensorimotor Approach to Psychotherapy
    (Norton Series on Interpersonal Neurobiology) P. Ogden, K. Minton, C.
    Pain - 2006 – W. W. Norton & Company.

18. Richard Bandler's Guide to Trance-formation; R Bandler – Deerfield Beach, FL: Health, 2008 – *hcibooks.com*

19. In Praise of the Incomplete Leader; Deborah Ancona, Thomas W. Malone, Wanda J. Orlikowski, and Peter M. Senge. Harvard Business School Publishing Corporation. 2007.

20. The Matrix Model, The Models of Neuro-Semantics, L. Michael Hall, Ph.D., *http://www.neurosemantics.com/ns-its-models/*

21. Aristotle, Ancient Greek philosopher

22. Personal Values Assessment is Copyright © 2017 under Cultural Transformation Tools® (CTT) and is a trademark of Barrett Values Centre, *https://survey.valuescentre.com/survey.html?id=s1TAEQUStmx-pUIle-ma6Q.*

23. NLP: Principles in Practice, Lisa Wake, 2010, p 22.

24. Paradoxical Thinking: How to Profit from Your Contradictions; Jerry Fletcher and Kelle Olwyler, (1997). San Francisco: Berrett-Koehler Publishers.

25. *https://bettermanblueprint.com/project328-framework-goal-setting-works/*

26. The 12 Week Year: Get More Done in 12 Weeks Than Others Do in 12 Months. Brian P. Moran and Michael Lennington.

27. Introduction to Outer Space. A Presidential Science Advisory Committee Pamphlet, published March 26, 1958. Author Unknown.

28. Expectancy Theory. Victor H. Vroom (1964), Yale School of Business.

29. Joseph John Campbell (March 26, 1904 – October 30, 1987), The Hero with a Thousand Faces.

30. Raven, Bertram H. (1992) "A power interaction model on interpersonal influence: French and Raven thirty years later". Journal of Social Behavior and Personality. Vol. 7, No. 2, 217-244

31. L. Michael Hall Ph.D., 2016 "Neurons" Meta Reflections – #52 November 7, 2016; Embrace the Fluidity of "Personality".

32. Songwriters L. Robin, J. Styne, Published by Lyrics © Music Sales Corporation, Song Discussions is protected by U.S. Patent 9401941. Other patents pending.

33. *http://agilemanifesto.org*

34. What Is Agile? (10 Key Principles of Agile) by Kelly Waters, February 10, 2007 | 10 Key Principles of Agile Development.

35. The Amplified Bible, Ecclesiastes 3:1-8, A Time for Everything.

36. Hersey, P. and Blanchard, K. H. (1969). Management of Organizational Behavior – Utilizing Human Resources. New Jersey/Prentice Hall.

- -

a. Baker, Dean (2009). Multi-Company Project Management: Maximizing Business Results through Strategic Collaboration. J Ross. p. 58.

b. What's in a Name? Integrating Homeostasis, Allostasis and Stress. Published in final edited form as: Horm Behav. 2010 Feb; 57(2): 105. Published online 2009, Sep 26. doi: *10.1016/j.yhbeh.2009.09.011*

c. Higher-Order Theories of Consciousness, an Anthology. Edited by Rocco J. Gennaro. John Benjamins Publishing Company Amsterdam/Philadelphia, Chapter 1.

d. *ism-journal.com/ITToday/projectfailure* by LA Kappelman, Fall 2006.

e. Salim Ismail (2014), Exponential Organisations, p 53. Diversion Books

f. Idris Mootee (2013), 60-Minute Brand Strategist: The Essential Brand Book for Marketing Professionals, p. 19. John Wiley & Sons.

g. *https://www.blueoceanstrategy.com*

h. Stephan May, Nigel Watts (2012), Write a Novel and Get Published (Teach yourself:writing).

i. Olds, J; Milner, P (December 1954). "Positive reinforcement produced by electrical stimulation of septal area and other regions of rat brain.". Journal of comparative and physiological psychology.

j. Fuster, J.M. The Prefrontal Cortex, (Raven Press, New York, 1997).

k. Taylor SB, Lewis CR, Olive MF (February 2013). "The neurocircuitry of illicit psychostimulant addiction: acute and chronic effects in humans".

l. Hewitt, John (26 March 2013). "Predicting repeat offenders with brain scans: You be the judge". *medicalxpress.com*

m. Wager, Tor (June 2002). "Functional Neuroanatomy of Emotion: A Meta-Analysis of Emotion Activation Studies in PET and fMRI"